# WARSHIPS

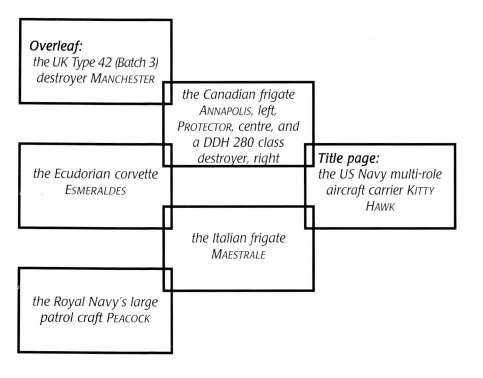

**Overleaf:**
the UK Type 42 (Batch 3)
destroyer MANCHESTER

the Canadian frigate
ANNAPOLIS, left,
PROTECTOR, centre, and
a DDH 280 class
destroyer, right

**Title page:**
the US Navy multi-role
aircraft carrier KITTY
HAWK

the Ecudorian corvette
ESMERALDES

the Italian frigate
MAESTRALE

the Royal Navy's large
patrol craft PEACOCK

# WARSHIPS

Caxton Editions

First published in Great Britain by
Caxton Editions
20 Bloomsbury Street
London WC1B 3JH

Unless credited to (Aldino), all of the photographs
in this publication have been supplied by courtesy of
TRH Pictures, London
**These pages:** *California and Virginia class cruisers of the US Navy*

ISBN 1 84067 319 2

Designed and produced by
Superlaunch Limited
PO Box 207
Abingdon
Oxfordshire OX13 6TA

Imagesetting by International Graphic Services, Bath
Printed and bound in Singapore

# CONTENTS

# INTRODUCTION

The warship types currently in existence or under construction are likely to remain substantially unchanged for perhaps a decade. However, during this time the future role of seapower requires serious re-examination. Since the end of the Cold War, a tendency to cut military spending has resulted in fewer ships being built. All over the world, those under construction tend to be smaller; a frigate is being built although the navy would have preferred a destroyer. We have seen also the promotion of smaller V/STOL carriers and the deployment of medium-sized amphibious ships with both helicopter and landing craft capabilities, under the pretext of pressure to maintain a balanced force. These cutbacks have all of the appearance of being logical; a smaller ship costs less to build and carries a smaller crew, which costs less to maintain, but this tendency may harm the effectiveness of the navy.

A decade ago, the Royal Navy aimed to have fifty surface combat vessels, but that figure has been progressively revised downwards. Although the UK has three new aircraft carriers planned to replace the existing force, these will not be commissioned until 2012. However, by then the navy's carrier-borne Sea Harriers should have been replaced by upgraded RAF Harriers, which in turn will eventually be replaced by the F35, under RAF control.

During the past half-century as our military focus has shifted away from central Europe and assumed threats from the east, the amalgamation and integration of our land, air and sea forces has ostensibly made sense. However, if they are to function as a single cohesive and potent military force no matter what the task, it must have an appropriate command structure. Likewise in order for the fleet to operate efficiently in size, usefulness and deployability, sufficient equipment of the highest standard must be available in quantity, and we await the costcutting to be replaced with investment in the tools to do the job.

The mighty US Navy's early twenty-first century structure indicates a navy comprising about 300 ships, but if building rates continue as at present, the size of the US fleet could be cut in half within a generation. While the capabilities and characteristics of different navies' battleships, cruisers, destroyers, submarines and aircraft carriers were closely similar throughout the years of the Second World War, the USA does have a huge advantage in that the current vessels have no equals. Today no other navy's carriers can match the Nimitz class, and no other nations's destroyers can match an Arleigh Burke class vessel.

# NOTES TO THE TEXT

This volume describes only surface vessels. They have been arranged alphabetically under each category, first by nation and then by class.

**Type:** aircraft carriers

CV: carriers generally including multi-role aircraft carriers

CVL: light aircraft carriers

CVLS: light aircraft carriers with sustainable ASW capabilities

CVG: carriers equipped with SAM guided missiles

CVH: carriers not fitted with arrest gear or catapults, but operating V/STOL/helicopters

CVN: as CV but nuclear-powered

CVS: as CVH but with sustainable ASW capabilities

Battleships BB, battleships generally

Cruisers CA: gun cruiser, main armament a 152.4mm (6in) or larger gun, no missiles

CC: general cruiser in excess of 150m (495ft)

CG: with guided missiles as main armament

CGN: as CG but nuclear-powered

Destroyers DD: destroyer type ship between 95–140m (313–462ft) long

DDG: armed with SAM guided missiles

Frigates FF: frigate type ships between 75–150m (247–495ft) long

FFG: armed with SAM guided missiles

FFH: with embarked helicopter

FFT: can also be used for training

Corvettes FS: small escort ship of between 60–100m (198–330ft)

FSG: armed with SAM guided missiles

FSH: with embarked helicopter

Patrol forces FAC: fast attack craft

PP: general patrol vessel

PG: general patrol vessel of between 45–85m (148–280ft) long with minimum 76mm (3in) armament, not designated to operate in open waters

PHM: high-speed (hydrofoil) craft with SSM capability

PT: high-speed (35kt) craft of between 20–30m (66–99ft) armed with anti-surface ship torpedoes

**Country:** where the ship is operated, not necessarily where it was built.

**Gun armament:** the figure (e.g. /70) following the gun size denotes the gun's calibre. The gun barrel length is determined by multiplying the inner diameter of the barrel by the calibre. Thus the 152.4mm (6in)/57 gun of the Soviet Sverdlov class cruisers has a length of 8,664mm (28.9ft approx).

**Complement:** where more than one overall figure is quoted, the first figure identifies the ships' officers; a second represents other ratings; the third and, where applicable the fourth, represent the air wing complement.

**Ships:** the number of ships in any class is identified first by the number commissioned. Where a class is too numerous to identify each vessel, only the first is named. The ship's pennant number is given in parentheses after the ship name.

# AIRCRAFT CARRIERS

The evolution of the jet aircraft during the second half of the twentieth century posed new problems for existing aircraft carriers, including the basic and essential issue of launch and recovery.

The jets were less capable than propellor-driven aircraft both of low speeds for landing and high acceleration for take-off from a carrier deck. Thus stronger arresting systems were needed to absorb the more powerful higher landing speeds, and unassisted take-offs were more or less out of the question. Another factor to be overcome was the jets' higher engine weight, which made necessary stronger, heavier airframes. This meant that the jets had higher fuel consumption and little more than half the airborne endurance of propellor-driven craft of comparable size. If more fuel were to be carried either performance would be reduced or the aircraft would have to be yet larger. This in turn would affect air group capacity while requiring longer, larger, stronger flight decks or even more powerful catapults.

The catapult launch itself was already found to slow down the assembly of an airborne strike force, with each aircraft requiring individual attention when manoeuvered onto the equipment. This problem could be overcome by the installation of multiple catapults, but this would increase the need for still bigger flight decks.

An F-4 Phantom prepares for take-off
from the deck of USS ENTERPRISE (Aldino)

Not only did aircraft carriers have to be bigger in order to achieve their primary function of deploying a fighter capability, but they also had to accommodate different types of aircraft: electronic countermeasures (ECM), early warning (AEW), tanker, and anti-submarine warfare (ASW).

Such necessary consideration of different aircraft types placed an increased strain on maintainance facilities and available space, and eventually led to the development of versatile multi-mission aircraft such as the F-4 Phantom and the more recent F/A-18 Hornet.

The advent of nuclear power for propulsion theoretically freed some internal space otherwise reserved for fuel oil, as well giving the carrier the increased range and speed. The craft was now able to endure hundreds of thousands of miles, for which it needed to be equipped with additional supplies and ordnance. Including more and increasingly sophisticated

electronic equipment also required a greater internal volume, as well as an above-deck proliferation of radar masts and dishes which could encroach on the fight deck area.

These increased demands, together with correspondingly increased capability, resulted in a downgrading of long-range batteries; the *USS Enterprise, illustrated below*, was commissioned in 1961 without any fixed

**Above:** *the KIEV, which entered service in 1975 as the largest Soviet ship in its fleet. The four carriers of the Kiev class had a complement of vertical take-off and landing (VTOL) Yakolev Yak-36 Forger strike fighters, but have been withdrawn from service and replaced by the single Modified Kiev class carrier*

battery, whether of guns or missiles. This may have resulted from the vast cost of producing, maintaining and operating such massive carriers; the USA is now the only country able to support a realistic attack carrier fleet. Its latest additions to be commissioned are the 81,600 ton Nimitz class ships.

The development of vertical and short take off and landing (V/STOL) aircraft, such as the British Aerospace Sea Harrier FRS1, has enabled smaller carriers to be constructed during the past twenty years. Examples include the 16,000 ton British Invincible class and the 15,000 ton Spanish Principe de Asturias class, while a yet smaller alternative, the Russian Moskva class with a complement of 18 Kaman Ka-25 helicopters, was developed for anti-submarine warfare.

# COLOSSUS CLASS

**Type:** aircraft carrier (CVLS)
**Country:** Brazil
**Displacement:** 15,890 tons normal and 19,900 tons full load
**Dimensions:** length 211.8m (696ft); beam 24.4m (80ft); draught 7.5m
(24.5ft); flight deck length 210.3m (690ft) and width 36.4m (119.6ft)
**Gun armament:** 10 Bofors 40mm (1.57in)
**Aircraft:** 6 Grumman S-2G Trackers, and up to 11 rotary-wing
**Electronics:** Lockheed SPS 40B air search radar, Plessey AWS 4 air/surface
search radar, 2 SPG fire-control radar, Signaal ZW 06 navigation radar
**Propulsion:** Parsons geared turbines; 4 Admiralty 3-drum boilers,
delivering 29,825kW (40,000shp) to two shafts
**Performance:** maximum speed 24kt
**Range:** 19320km (12,000 miles) at 14kt
**Complement:** 1,300 including small air group
**Ships:** one, *Minas Gerais* (A11), ex British Colossus class HMS *Vengeance*

*Below: HMS Vengeance which was laid down in 1942 and commissioned into
the British fleet in 1945. In 1953 it was loaned to the RAN initially as a training
carrier, before being refitted as a front-line fleet carrier. It was sold to Brazil in
1956 and extensively modified before commissioning in 1960*

# CHARLES DE GAULLE CLASS

**Type:** aircraft carrier (CVN)
**Country:** France
**Displacement:** 36,600 tons normal and 39,680 tons full load
**Dimensions:** length 261.5m (857.7ft); beam 31.8m (104.3ft); draught 8.5m (27.8ft); flight deck length 261.5m (857.7ft) and width 64.4m (211.3ft)
**Gun armament:** 8 Giat 20F2 20mm (0.79in)
**Missile armament:** 4 EUROSAM VLS octupal SSM launchers and 2 Matra Sadral PDMS sextupal SAM launchers
**Aircraft:** up to 40 fixed-wing including Rafale(M), *below, landing on the carrier*; Super Étendards; E-2C Hawkeye AEW and AS 565 Panther helicopters
**Electronics:** Thomson-CSF DRBJ 11 D/E and 26D air search radar, Thomson-CSF DRBV 15C air/surface search radar, Arabel I/J band fire-control radar, two Racal 1229 navigation radar, SLAT torpedo-warning sonar
**Propulsion:** two Type K15 pressurised water-cooled reactors supplying steam to two sets of geared turbines delivering 61,150kW (82,015shp) to two shafts
**Performance:** maximum speed 27kt
**Complement:** 1,150 and and air group of 550
**Ships:** one, *Charles de Gaulle* (R91)
**Remarks:** although laid down in 1989, the ship encountered many problems during her sea trials

# CLÉMENCEAU CLASS

**Type:** aircraft carrier (CV)
**Country:** France
**Displacement:** 27,310 tons normal and 32,780 tons full load
**Dimensions:** length 265m (869.4ft); beam 31.72m (104.1ft); draught 8.6m (28.2ft); flight deck length 257m (843.2ft) and width 29.5m (96.8ft)
**Gun armament:** eight 100mm (3.94in) L/55 DP in single mountings
**Missile armament:** two Thomson-CSF Crotale EDIR SAM launchers
**Aircraft:** 37 fixed-wing (18 Dassault-Breguet Super Étendards, 4 Étendard IVPs, 8 Vought F-8 Crusaders and 7 Dassault-Breguet Alizes), and two SA 365F Dauphin 2 helicopters
**Electronics:** Thomson-CSF DRBV 23B air search radar; two Thomson-CSF DRBI 10 and one DRBV 15 air/surface search radar; two Thomson-CSF DRBC 32B and two Crotale fire-control radars, Racal Decca 1226 navigation radar, NRBA 51 landing approach control radar, Westinghouse SQS-505 hull-mounted sonars
**Propulsion:** six boilers supplying steam to two sets of Parsons geared turbines delivering 93,960kW (126,000shp) to two shafts
**Performance:** maximum speed 32kt
**Range:** 12,000km (7,500 miles) at 18kts
**Complement:** 64 + 476 + 798
**Ships:** two; *Clémenceau* (R98) and *Foch* (R99)
**Remarks:** commissioned in the early 1960s, both ships were later modernised to equip them for the nuclear-capable Super Étendard fighter-bombers. *Foch, illustrated below*, was recently sold to Brazil

# HERMES CLASS

**Type:** aircraft carrier (CV)
**Country:** India
**Displacement:** 23,900 tons standard and 28,700 tons full load
**Dimensions:** length 208.8m (685ft); beam 27.4m (90ft); draught 8.7m
(28.5ft); flight deck length 226.9m (744.3ft) and width 30.48m (100ft)
**Gun armament:** some 30mm (1.18in) ADGs may be fitted
**Missile armament:** two Short's Seacat SAM launchers
**Aircraft:** maximum 37 aircraft, usually twelve Sea Harriers FRS Mk 51 and
seven Sea King Mk 42B/C helicopters
**Electronics:** Marconi Type 996 air-search radar, Plessey Type 994 air/
surface-search radar, 2 Racal Decca 1006 navigation radars, 2 Plessey
Type 904 fire-control systems, Graseby Type 184M hull-mounted sonars
**Propulsion:** four Admiralty boilers supplying steam to two sets of Parsons
geared turbines delivering 56,675kW (76,000shp) to two shafts
**Performance:** maximum speed 28kt
**Range:** 9,660km (6,000 miles) at 20kt
**Complement:** 143 + 1,207 including air group
**Ships:** one, *Viraat* (R22), ex British Centaur class HMS *Hermes*
**Remarks:** built by Vickers-Armstrong at Barrow, *Hermes* was
commissioned in 1959; during the mid-1970s she was modified as an
interim ASW ship, which is how she is *illustrated below*. This included the
addition of the ski-jump at the bows. While still in British hands, *Hermes*
operated as the flagship for the Falklands Task Force in 1982 and
received a minor refit before being sold to the Indian Navy

# MAJESTIC CLASS

**Type:** aircraft carrier (CVL)
**Country:** India
**Displacement:** 16,000 tons standard and 19,550 tons full load
**Dimensions:** length 213.4m (700ft); beam 24.4m (80ft); draught 7.3m (24ft); flight deck length 210m (690ft) and width 34m (112ft)
**Gun armament:** seven Bofors 40mm (1.57in); 30mm (1.18in) ADGs may be fitted as replacements
**Aircraft:** six Sea Harriers FRS Mk 51; nine Sea King Mk 42 ASW/ASV and one Chetak SAR helicopter
**Electronics:** Signaal LW 08 air-search radar, Signaal DA 05 air/surface-search radar, Signaal ZW 06 navigation radar, Graseby 750 hull-mounted sonars
**Propulsion:** four Admiralty 3-drum boilers supplying steam to Parsons geared turbines delivering 31,316kW (42,000shp) to two shafts
**Performance:** maximum speed 24.5kt
**Range:** 19,320km (12,000 miles) at 14kt
**Complement:** 1,343 including air group
**Ships:** one, *Vikrant* (R11), ex British Majestic class HMS *Hercules*
**Remarks:** the last of the Majestic class vessels to be completed, *Hercules* was built by Vickers-Armstrong at Newcastle and launched in 1945. The ship was then laid up for ten years before being purchased by the Indian Government in January 1957. The *Vikrant* saw combat in the 1971 war with Pakistan, was refitted 1979, and again refitted in 1982. There is a 9.75 ski-jump, but no angled flight deck, and her small island is on the starboard side forward of midships

# GARIBALDI CLASS

**Type:** aircraft carrier  (CVLS)
**Country:** Italy
**Displacement:** 10,100 tons standard and 13,370 tons full load
**Dimensions:** length 180m (590.4ft); beam 33.4m (110.2ft); draught 6.7m
(22ft); flight deck length 174m (570.7ft) and width 30.4m (99.7ft)
**Gun armament:** six 40mm (1.57in) Breda L/70 AA in three twin mountings
**Missile armament:** two Twin Teseo launchers for 10 Otomat Mk 2 surface-to-
surface missiles, and two Albatros launchers for Aspide surface-to-air missiles
**Anti-submarine armament:** two triple ILAS 3 tube mountings for 324mm
(12.75in) A244S or 324mm (12.75in) Mk 46 A6S torpedoes
**Aircraft:** 16 AV-8B Harrier IIs or 18 Agusta-Sikorsky SH-3D Sea King helicopters
**Electronics:** Hughes SPS 52C and 3D long range air-search radar, Selenia
SPS 768 (RAN 3L) and SMA SPN 728 air-search radar, Selenia SPS 774
(RAN 10S) air/surface-search radar, SMA SPS 702 UPX and 718 beacon
surface search/target indication radar, SMA SPN 749(V)2 navigation
radars, 3 Selenia SPG 75 (RTN 30X) and 3 Selenia SPG 74 (RTN 20X)  fire-
control systems, Raytheon DE 1160 LF bow-mounted sonars
**Propulsion:** four General Electric-Fiat LM2500 gas turbines delivering
59,655kW (80,000shp) to two shafts
**Performance:** maximum speed 30kt
**Range:** 11,270km (7,000 miles) at 20kt
**Complement:** 550 (accommodation is available for 825)
**Ships:** one, *Guiseppe Garibaldi* (C551) (another is due to be launched in 2007)
**Remarks:** laid down in March 1981, she entered service in October 1985

# KIEV (MODIFIED) CLASS

**Type:** aircraft carrier (CV)
**Country:** Russia and associated states
**Displacement:** 44,500 tons full load
**Dimensions:** length 273m (895.7ft); beam 51m (167.3ft); draught 10m (32.8ft); flight deck length 195m (640ft) and width 20.7m (68ft)
**Gun armament:** two 100mm (3.94in) L/70 DP in single mountings and eight 30mm (1.18in) ADGM 630 CIWS mountings
**Missile armament:** six twin container-launchers for 12 SS-N-12 Sandbox SSM missiles and four groups of sextuple vertical launchers for 4 SA-N-9 SAMs
**Aircraft:** 12 fixed-wing V/STOL; 19 Ka-27 Helix A and 3 Ka-25 Hormone B helicopters
**Electronics:** Sky Watch, 4 Planar phased array and 3D air-search radar, Plate Steer air/surface search radar, 2 Strut Pair surface search radar, 3 Palm Frond navigation radar, fire-control and aircraft control radar and Horse Jaw hull-mounted sonar
**Propulsion:** eight boilers supplying steam to four sets of geared turbines delivering 150,000kW (201,180shp) to four shafts
**Performance:** maximum speed 32kt
**Range:** 21,750km (13,500 miles) at 18kt
**Complement:** 1,200 excluding air group
**Ships:** one, *Admiral Gorshkov* (ex *Baku*)
**Remarks:** *Admiral Gorshkov* carries considerably more electronics and armaments which are also of a much improved quality, than the original Kiev class carriers (*Aldino*)

# KUZNETSOV CLASS

**Type:** aircraft carrier (CVN)
**Country:** Russia and associated states
**Displacement:** 67,500 tons full load
**Dimensions:** length 280m (918.6ft); beam 37m (121.4ft); draught 10.5m (34.4ft); flight deck length 304.5m (999ft) and width 70m (229.7ft)
**Gun armament:** six 30mm (1.18in) AK 630 with 6 barrels per mounting
**Missile armament:** twelve SS-N-19 Shipwreck SSM launchers; four SA-N-9 sextuple SAM vertical launchers; eight CADS-N-1 SAM/Guns each with twin 30mm (1.18in) Gatling combined with 8 SA-N-11 and Hot Flush/Hot Spot fire control radar/optronic director
**Anti-submarine armament:** 2 RBU 12000 mortars
**Aircraft:** twenty Su-27K Flanker D and four Su-25 UTG Frogfoot fixed wing aircraft; 15 Ka-27 Helix and 3 Ka-29 Helix AEW helicopters
**Electronics:** Sky Watch and 3D air-search radar, Top Plate air/surface search radar, 2 Strut Pair surface search radar, 3 Palm Frond navigation radar, 4 Cross Sword fire-control and Fly Trap B aircraft control radar and Horse Jaw hull-mounted sonar
**Performance:** maximum speed 30kt
**Ships:** two; *Admiral Kuznetsov* (ex *Tbilisi,* ex *Leonid Brezhnev*), *Varyag* (ex *Riga*)

*Below: the multi-role hybrid carrier* ADMIRAL KUZNETSOV *has a typically high, sweeping bow profile and a 12  ski-ramp*

# PRINCIPE DE ASTURIAS CLASS

**Type:** aircraft carrier (CVL)
**Country:** Spain
**Displacement:** 17,188 tons full load
**Dimensions:** length 195.9m (642.7ft); beam 24.3m (79.7ft); draught 9.4m (30.8ft); flight deck length 175.3m (575ft) and width 29m (95.1ft)
**Gun armament:** four Bazán Meroka 12-barrelled 20mm (0.79in); two Rheinmetall 37mm (1.46in) saluting guns
**Aircraft:** six 12 AV 8B Harrier V/STOL fixed wing aircraft; six 10 SH-3 Sea King and two SH-60B Seahawk helicopters
**Electronics:** Hughes SPS 52C/D and 3D long range air-search radar, ISC Cardion SPS 55 surface-search radar, one Selenia RAN 12L, four Sperry VPS 2 and one TRN 11L/X fire-control systems, ITT SPN 35A aircraft control radar
**Propulsion:** two General Electric LM2500 gas turbines delivering 29,825kW (40,000shp) to a single shaft
**Performance:** maximum speed 26kt
**Range:** 10,500km (6,500 miles) at 20kt
**Complement:** 774 excluding air group
**Ships:** one, *Principe de Asturias* (R11), ex *Almirante Carrero Blanco*
**Remarks:** in order to build their only remaining carrier, it was necessary for the Spanish Government to negotiate considerable US assistance, both technical and financial. The carrier was ordered in 1977, laid down in 1979, but not commissioned until 1988

*An artist's impression of the United Kingdom's 'New Carrier', two of which have been ordered for commissioning in 2010/2012. At 40,000–50,000 tons with a capacity for sixty aircraft including six helicopters and four early warning aircraft, and a total crew of 1,200 personnel, they will be larger than the three existing Invincible class carriers which they will replace (Aldino)*

# INVINCIBLE CLASS

**Type:** aircraft carrier (CVLS)
**Country:** United Kingdom
**Displacement:** 16,256 tons standard and 20,600 tons full load
**Dimensions:** length 209.1m (685.8ft); beam 36m (118ft); draught 8m (26ft); flight deck length 167.8m (550ft) and width 13.5m (44.3ft)
**Gun armament:** three GE/GD 20mm (0.79in) Mk 15 Vulcan Phalanx; three Signaal/GE 30mm (1.18in) Gatling Gamekeeper; two Oerlikon/ BMARC 20mm (0.79in) GAM/BO1
**Missile armament:** one twin launcher for 22 Sea Dart surface-to-air missiles
**Aircraft:** nine BAe Sea Harrier FRS Mk 1/2 V/STOL aircraft; nine Westland Sea King HAS 6 and three Westland Sea King AEW 2 helicopters
**Propulsion:** four Rolls-Royce Olympus TM3B gas turbines delivering 83,520kW (112,000shp) to two shafts
**Performance:** maximum speed 28kt
**Range:** 11,250km (7,000 miles) at 19kt
**Complement:** 131 + 131 + 869 + 284 air group personnel
**Ships:** three; *Invincible* (R 05), *Illustrious* (R 06) and, *illustrated below, Ark Royal* (R 07)

# ENTERPRISE CLASS

**Type:** aircraft carrier (CVN)
**Country:** United States of America
**Displacement:** 75,700 tons standard and 93,970 tons full load
**Dimensions:** length 342.3m (1,123ft); beam 40.5m (133ft); draught 11.9m (39ft); flight deck length 331.6m (1,088ft) and flight deck width 76.8m (252ft)
**Gun armament:** three GE/GD Vulcan Phalanx Mk 15 20mm (0.79in)
**Missile armament:** three Raytheon GMSL Mk 29 launchers for SAMs
**Aircraft:** about 78 including F14 Tomcat, F/A-18 Hornet, EA-6B Prowler, A-6E Intruder, E-C2 Hawkeye and S-3A/B Viking fixed wing; SH-3G/H Sea King and SH-60F Seahawk helicopters
**Electronics:** surface and air search radar, aircraft landing radar, missile fire control and navigation radar
**Propulsion:** eight pressurised water-cooled Westinghouse A2W reactors supplying steam to four sets of Westinghouse geared turbines delivering 208,795kW (280,000shp) to four shafts
**Performance:** maximum speed 33kt
**Range:** 741,245km (460,600 miles)
**Complement:** 162 + 2,940, and a carrier air-wing complement of 304 + 2,323
**Ships:** one, *Enterprise* (CVN 65). Commissioned in 1961. the ship served in sustained operations off Vietnam in several tours from 1965 onwards

# KITTY HAWK CLASS

**Type:** aircraft carrier (CV)
**Country:** United States of America
The following specifications refer to *Kitty Hawk*, which was commissioned in 1961 as an improved Forrestal class carrier
**Displacement:** 60,100 tons standard and 81,123 tons full load
**Dimensions:** length 323.6m (1,062.5ft); beam 39.6m (130ft); draught 11.4m (37.4ft); flight deck length 318.8m (1,046ft) and width 76.8m (252ft)
**Gun armament:** three 20mm (0.79in) Vulcan Phalanx Mk 15
**Missile armament:** three Mk 29 octuple launchers for Sea Sparrow SAMs
**Aircraft:** about 78, comprising same types and range as Enterprise class
**Electronics:** air-search radar, surface search radar, navigation radar, missile fire-control systems,  height-finding radar. CV 66 and CV 67 fitted with SQS 23 sonar
**Propulsion:** eight Foster-Wheeler boilers supplying steam to four sets of Westinghouse geared turbines delivering 208,795kW (208,000shp) to four shafts
**Performance:** maximum speed 32kt
**Range:** 19,320km (12,000 miles) at 20kt
**Complement:** 150 + 2,645, and air wing complement of about 2,150
**Ships:** four; *Kitty Hawk* (CV 63) *illustrated below, Constellation* (CV 64), *America* (CV 63) and *John F Kennedy* (CV 67)

# NIMITZ CLASS

**Type:** aircraft carrier (CVN)
**Country:** United States of America
The following specifications refer to *George Washington*, which is the world's largest aircraft carrier
**Displacement:** 81,600 tons standard and 102,000 tons full load
**Dimensions:** length 317m (1,040ft); beam 40.8m (134ft); draught 11.9m (39ft); flight deck length 332.9m (1,092ft) and width 76.8m (252ft); angled flight deck 237.7m (779.8ft)
**Gun armament:** four 20mm (0.79in) Vulcan Phalanx Mk 15
**Missile armament:** three Mk 29 launchers for 24 RIM-7 Sea Sparrow SAMs
**Aircraft:** up to 76 fixed wing, and 8 helicopters
**Propulsion:** two pressurised-water cooled nuclear reactors (Westinghouse A4W or General Electric A1G) supplying steam to four sets of geared turbines delivering 193,880kW (260,000shp) to four shafts
**Performance:** maximum speed 30+kt
**Complement:** 3,300 and a carrier air wing strength of 2,800
**Ships:** eight; *Nimitz* (CVN 68) *illustrated below*, *Dwight D Eisenhower* (CVN 69), *Carl Vinson* (CVN 70), *Theodore Roosevelt* (CVN 71), *Abraham Lincoln* (CVN 72), *George Washington* (CVN 73), including the two being built, *John C Stennis* (CVN 74) and *United States* (CVN 75)

# HELICOPTER CARRIERS

Sometimes known as helicopter cruisers, helicopter carriers are basically anti-submarine warfare ships, epitomised by the *Moskva*, which was the first Russian attempt to build a significant air-capable ship. She was laid down in 1962, and designed to counter the US Polaris submarines operating in the eastern Mediterranean. The French vessel, *Jeanne d'Arc*, by then had already been launched as an ASW/assault ship. Both of these vessels have the superstructure concentrated forward, with the after half of the decks given over to a flight deck. In the case of the *Moskva, illustrated below*, the hull of the vessel is faired up at the edges, thus producing a unique tear-drop shape.

# JEANNE D'ARC CLASS

**Type:** aircraft carrier (CVLS)
**Country:** France
**Displacement:** 10,000 tons normal and 13,270 tons full load
**Dimensions:** length 182m (597.1ft); beam 24m (78.7ft); draught 7.3m
(24ft); flight deck length 62m 203.4ft) and width 21m (68.9ft)
**Gun armament:** four DCN 100mm (3.94in) L/55 DP in single mountings
**Missile armament:** six Aerospatiale MM 38 Exocet SSM
**Aircraft:** four SA 365F Dauphin 2 helicopters (eight in wartime, including
Super Pumas and Lynx)
**Electronics:** Thomson-CSF DRBV 22D air search radar; Thomson-CSF
DRBV 51 air/surface search radar; three Thomson-CSF DRBC 32A fire-
control radars, Racal Decca 1226 DRBN navigation radar, Thomson Sintra
DUBV 24C hull-mounted sonars
**Propulsion:** six multi-tubular boilers supplying steam to Rateau-Bretagne
geared turbines delivering 29,825kW (40,000shp) to two shafts
**Performance:** maximum speed 26.5kt
**Range:** 9,660km (6,000 miles) at 15kts
**Complement:** 1,050 including small air group
**Ships:** one, *Jeanne d'Arc* (R97), ex *La Résolue*
**Remarks:** commissioned in 1964; the Exocet launchers were added in a
1975 refit, and the vessel was refitted again in 1982. The superstructure
of the vessel is concentrated forward

# MOSKVA CLASS

**Type:** helicopter carrier (CVS)
**Country:** Russia and associated states
**Displacement:** 14,500 tons standard and 18,000 tons full load
**Dimensions:** length 190.5m (624ft); beam 34.14m (112ft); draught 7.6m (25ft); flight deck length 81m (265.7ft) and width 33m (108ft)
**Gun armament:** four 57mm (2.24in) L/70 AA
**Missile armament:** two twin launchers for 48 SA-N-3 and 'Goblet' surface-to-air missiles
**Anti-submarine armament:** one twin SUW-N-1 launcher for 20 FRAS-1 missiles, two RBU 6000 12-barrel rocket launchers and helicopter-launched weapons

**Aircraft:** 18 Kamov Ka-25 Hormone-A ASW helicopters
**Electronics:** one 'Top Sail' 3D radar, one 'Head Net-C' 3D radar, two 'Head Light' SAM-control radars, two 'Muff Cob' AA gun-control radars and three 'Don-2' navigation radars
**Propulsion:** four boilers supplying steam to two sets of geared turbines delivering 74,570kW (100,000shp) to two shafts
**Performance:** maximum speed 30kt
**Range:** 16,675km (10,360 miles) at 18kt or 5,200km (3,230 miles) at 30kt
**Complement:** 840 excluding all group personnel
**Ships:** two; *Moskva* and *Leningrad*

*Below:* MOSKVA *in 1969 on exercises in the Mediterranean Sea with Ka-25 Hormone helicopters on her aft deck*

# BATTLESHIPS

*USS Missouri firing her guns during operation Desert Storm (Aldino)*

The US Iowa class battleship *Missouri* was the last active battleship in the world; however, she was decommissioned on 31 March 1992, and now lies in reserve. She last saw action in 1991 in the Persian Gulf for Operation Desert Storm, together with her sister ship *Wisconsin*, but battleships have now effectively passed from the scene, relics of the era when the big gun held sway at sea.

The capital ship had developed in the second half of the nineteenth century, when the skills of the ironmasters were able to achieve feats of extraordinary engineering, culminating in the *Dreadnaught* of 1907. As bigger guns supposedly gave more protection, so ships were built with the ability to pound each other to scrap metal.

After the First World War there was an international agreement which imposed limitations on the use of both guns and armour. Both Japan and the United States, by 1920, were already laying down large battleships and battlecruisers with displacements as high as 43,000 tons and mounting 406mm (16in) guns. Britain drew up plans for similar ships, but in the inter-war years built only *Hood*, which had been laid down in 1916, and completed two Nelson class ships in 1927. Five King George V ships were laid down and completed between 1940–42, then only one further British battleship was built, *Vanguard*, completed in 1946 and scrapped in 1960.

Germany launched seven battleships during the 1930s, including the Deutschland class *Admiral Graf Spee*. She had a side belt 80mm (3.15in) thick, increasing to 100mm (3.94in) forward and aft where the main magazine spaces were located. Two Scharnhorst class ships were capable of 32kts and armed with nine 280mm (11.02in), twelve 150mm (5.9in), ten 105mm (4.13in),

twelve 37mm (1.46in) and ten 20mm (0.79in) guns; the largest battleships, the Bismarck class *Bismarck* and *Tirpitz*, had respectively displacements of 41,700 and 42,367 tons standard, and 50,900 and 51,714 tons full load.

The ultimate Japanese battleships were the Yamato class ships, of which two were completed, the *Yamato* in 1941 and the *Musashi* in 1942. *Yamato* fired her main armament for the first and only time against US surface targets on 25 October 1944 and was sunk on 7 April 1945 after being hit by eleven torpedoes and eight bombs in the space of seventy-five minutes.

Although the Soviet Union began production of battleships during the inter-war years, none was ever commissioned. The United States thought big, however, building ships that were capable of survival and endurance, decked out with big guns. Speed was temporarily a secondary consideration but when speed was deemed necessary, it simply built bigger ships.

At the end of the First World War, it had in the yards the three New Mexico class ships (which were rebuilt in 1933) and two Tennessee class ships (rebuilt in 1943). These were followed by three Colorado class ships that were completed in the early 1920s. During the years of the Second World War it completed two North Carolina class, four South Dakota class and the four Iowa class ships, since when battleship construction has ceased.

# IOWA CLASS

**Type:** battleship (BB)
**Country:** United States of America
**Displacement:** 48,110 tons standard and 57,540 tons full load
**Dimensions:** length 270.4m (887.2ft); beam 33m (108.2); draught 8.84m (29ft)
**Gun armament:** *Iowa*, as built, nine 406mm (16in), twenty 127mm (5in) eighty 40mm (1.57in) and forty-nine 20mm (0.79in)
**Missile armament:** added to *Iowa* in 1984, 32 Tomahawk land attack and anti-ship cruise missiles and 16 Harpoon anti-ship missiles
**Aircraft:** provision for 3–4 helicopters on aft platform
**Electronics:** long-range air-search, medium-range air/surface search and navigation radars; gun directors controlled by fire-control system
**Propulsion:** eight Babcock & Wilcox boilers supplying steam to four sets of geared turbines delivering 158,090kW (212,000shp) to four shafts
**Performance:** maximum speed 33kt
**Range:** 27,800km (17,275 miles) at 17kt
**Complement:** 1,921
**Ships:** four; *Iowa* (BB61), *New Jersey* (BB62), *Missouri* (BB63), *Wisconsin* (BB64)

# CRUISERS

*Ticonderoga class vessel Vincennes (CG49) fires a Honeywell RUR-5A ASROC anti-submarine missile*

Historically the cruiser varied in size from just a few hundred tons, with guns smaller than those of a traditional destroyer, to the very potent warship of over 40,000 tons, larger than most battleships, armed with 381mm (15in) guns. During this time the cruiser has been categorised as battle cruiser first, second, third-class, armoured, torpedo and scout, but since the 1960s designated only as light or heavy.

The mission of the cruiser has also varied widely from that of lone operations and patrols, to scouting and convoy protection. It developed into the workhorse of the fleet during the First World War, a vital component of naval operations during the Second World War, and the capital surface warship during the Cold War period. In this way, cruisers changed the perception of the naval balance in the 1960s.

However, since then, only Russia has laid down any new gun cruisers, the large 13,600 ton fourteen-strong Sverdlov class, mounted with 152.4mm (6in) guns. By the time of their appearance the gun age was rapidly making way for the missile age, and the USA had already converted two heavy cruisers to guided missile cruisers, and more conversions followed in the 1960s which extended the life of these cruisers by a further twenty years.

During the late 1970s, Russia commissioned the battle cruiser *Kirov*, as an answer to what the West had considered to be the last of the true cruisers, USS *Long Beach*. This 15,100 ton vessel was the first nuclear-powered surface combatant, and originally her weaponry consisted of three missile launchers but no guns, although two 127mm (5in) guns were added later. In May 1968 during action in the Vietnam War, *Long Beach* was the first ship to be credited with shooting down aircraft with SAMs.

*Long Beach* had been commissioned just one year ahead of the completion

**Above:** *the Soviet navy's* ZHDANOV *(875), a Sverdlov class cruiser photographed in 1973, and* **below,** LONG BEACH *(CGN9), which was designed primarily for the air defence of carrier battle groups*

of the Russian Kynda class rocket cruiser, of which four were built. These were followed by the larger Kresta I class in 1967, and the Kresta II (*below*) anti-submarine warfare ships. These started to appear in 1970, and were designated BPKs. They were followed by the seven-ship Kara class to complete a very potent blue-water cruiser navy with which the Soviet could challenge the West. The American response was the redesignation, in 1975, of twenty-two guided missile frigates, and conventionally-powered guided missile cruisers, into a nine-ship Leahy class, nine-ship Belknap class, the single *Truxton*, two California class and four Virginia class vessels that had all been recommissioned by the end of the 1970s.

Although Italy, France and Great Britain all built cruisers after the Second World War, only America and Russia enacted serious building programmes. In the 1980s both countries launched interesting types, Russia producing the Sovremenny, Udaloy and Kirov classes. The latter, armed with five different missile systems, three gun systems and a trio of helicopters, were the largest surface combatants to be built anywhere in the second half of the century. America built the formidable Ticonderoga class, equipped with highly sophisticated electronics, two 127mm (5in) guns and two helicopters, in order to counter this Soviet threat.

# VITTORIO VENETO CLASS

**Type:** cruiser (CG)
**Country:** Italy
**Displacement:** 7,500 tons standard and 9,500 tons full load
**Dimensions:** length 179.6m (589ft); beam 19.4m (63.3ft); draught 6m (19.7ft)
**Gun armament:** eight OTO Melara 76mm (3in)/62 MMK and six Breda 40mm (1.57in)/70
**Missile armament:** four OTO Melara Teseo Mk 2 SSMs; GDC Pomona Standard SM-1ER and Aster twin Mk 10 Mod 9 SAM launcher; Honeywell A/S ASROC launcher
**Anti-submarine armament:** six 324mm (12.75in) US Mk 32 tubes; Honeywell Mk 46 torpedoes
**Aircraft:** six AB 212ASW helicopters
**Electronics:** long range air-search, air-search, surface-search with target indication, navigation, fire-control systems and sonars
**Propulsion:** four Ansaldo/Foster-Wheeler boilers supplying steam to two sets of geared turbines delivering 54,500kW (73,095shp) to two shafts
**Performance:** maximum speed 32kt
**Range:** 9,250km (5,750 miles) at 17kt
**Complement:** 50 + 500
**Ships:** one, *Vittorio Veneto* (C 550)

# DE RUYTER CLASS

**Type:** cruiser (CA)
**Country:** Peru
**Displacement:** 12,165 tons full load
**Dimensions:** length 185.6m (609ft); beam 17.3m (56.7ft); draught 6.7m (22ft)
**Gun armament:** eight Bofors 152.4mm (6in)/53
**Missile armament:** eight Aerospatiale MM 38 Exocet SSMs
**Aircraft:** three Agusta ASH-3D Sea King helicopters on *Aguirre* only
**Electronics:** air-search, surface-search with target indication, navigation, fire-control systems and hull-mounted sonars
**Performance:** maximum speed 32kt
**Range:** 11,270km (7,000 miles) at 12kt
**Ships:** two; *Almirante Grau* (CH 81), ex HrMs *De Ruyter*; and *Aguirre* (CH 84), ex HrMs *De Zeven Provincien*. The above details refer to *Almirante Grau*

# KARA CLASS

**Type:** cruiser (CG)
**Country:** Russia and associated states
**Displacement:** 8,200 tons standard and 9,900 tons full load
**Dimensions:** length 173.2m (568ft); beam 18.6m (61ft); draught 6.7m (22ft)
**Gun armament:** four 76mm (3in)/60 in twin mountings and four 30mm (1.18in)/65 with six barrels per mounting
**Missile armament:** two SA-N-3, six SA-N-6 and two SA-N-4 SAM launchers; two SS-N-14 quad A/S launchers
**Torpedo armament:** two quintuple 533mm (21in) tube mountings
**Anti-submarine armament:** two RBU 6,000 12-barrel rocket launchers; two RBU 1,000 six-barrel rocket launchers
**Aircraft:** one Kamov KA-25 Hormone-A helicopter
**Electronics:** air-search, air/surface-search, navigation, fire-control systems and hull-mounted sonars
**Propulsion:** COGOG (COmbined Gas Or Gas turbine) arrangement, with two gas turbines delivering 17,900kW (24,000shp) and four gas turbines delivering 74,570kW (100,000shp) to two shafts
**Performance:** maximum speed 34kt
**Range:** 14,500km (9,000 miles) at 15kt
**Complement:** 30 + 510
**Ships:** five; *Ochakov, Kerch, Azov, Petropavlovsk, Vladivostok* (ex *Tallinn*)

# **KIROV** CLASS

**Type:** cruiser (CGN)
**Country:** Russia and associated states
**Displacement:** 19,000 tons standard and 24,300 tons full load
**Dimensions:** length 252m (826.8ft); beam 28.5m (93.5ft); draught 9.1m (29.5ft)
**Gun armament:** two 100mm (3.94in) and eight 30mm (1.18in) mountings
**Missile armament:** 20 launch tubes for SS-N-19 SSMs; twelve SA-N-6, and
two twin SA-N-4 and two SA-N-9 octuple lunch tubes for SAMs
**Torpedo armament:** ten 533mm (21in) type 53 tube mountings
**Anti-submarine armament:** twin launcher for SS-N-14 'Silex' A/S missiles,
and RBU 6000 A/S mortars
**Aircraft:** three Kamov KA-25 Hormone-A or Ka-27 Helix helicopters on a
platform aft
**Electronics:** air search; air/surface search; navigation radars; fire control;
hull-mounted sonars and electronic countermeasures
**Propulsion:** two nuclear reactors with boilers supplying steam to turbines
delivering 119,300kW (160,000shp)
**Performance:** maximum speed 30kt
**Range:** 8,695km (14,000 miles) at 30kt
**Complement:** 900
**Ships:** four; *Admiral Ushakov* (ex *Kirov*), *Admiral Lazarev* (ex *Frunze*), *Admiral
Nakhimov* (ex *Kalinin*) and *Pyotr Velikiy* (ex *Yuri Andropov*)
**Remarks:** *Pyotr Velikiy* (Peter the Great), *illustrated below*, acted as a target
for the submarine *Kursk*'s test firing manoeuvres at the time of the
submarine's disaster in August 2000 (Aldino)

# SLAVA CLASS

**Type:** cruiser (CG)
**Country:** Russia and associated states
**Displacement:** 11,200 tons full load
**Dimensions:** length 186m (610.2ft); beam 20.8m (68.2ft); draught 7.6m (24.9ft)
**Gun armament:** two 130mm (5.1in)/70; six 30mm (1.18in)/65 mountings
**Missile armament:** sixteen SS-N-12 SSM launch tubes; eight SA-N-6 and two twin SA-N-4 SAM launchers
**Torpedo armament:** ten 533mm (21in) type 53 tube mountings
**Anti-submarine armament:** two RBU 6000 12-tubed mortars
**Aircraft:** one Kamov KA-25 Hormone B helicopter
**Electronics:** air search; air/surface search; navigation; fire control radars, and hull-mounted sonars and electronic countermeasures
**Performance:** maximum speed 32kt
**Range:** 9,660km (6,000 miles) at 15kt
**Ships:** four; *Slava, illustrated below,* which was originally designated as a Krasina class cruiser; *Marshal Ustinov, Chervona Ukraina,* and *Vilna Ukraina* (ex *Admiral Lobov*)

# TICONDEROGA CLASS

**Type:** cruiser (CG)
**Country:** United States of America
**Displacement:** 9,600 tons full load
**Dimensions:** length 172.8m (566.8ft); beam 16.8m (55ft);
draught 9.5m (31ft)
**Gun armament:** two 127mm (5in)/54 Mk 45 single mountings; two
20mm (0.79in)/76 Phalanx Mk 15 close-in weapon system mountings
**Missile armament:** two octuple container-launchers for 16 RGM-84A
Harpoon SSMs and two Mk 26 Mod 5 twin launchers for up to 68
RIM-67B Standard SAMs; ships from CG 52 onwards have two EX 41
vertical launchers in place of the Mk 26 launchers for up to 122 assorted
missiles, and two VLS each with 12 BGM-109 Tomahawk SLCMs
**Anti-submarine armament:** two triple Mk 32 tube mountings for 324mm
(12.75in) Mk 46 A/S torpedoes, up to 20 Honeywell ASROC missiles
**Aircraft:** two Sikorsky SH-60B Seahawk helicopters
**Propulsion:** four General Electric LM 2500 gas turbines delivering
59,655kW (80,000shp) to two shafts
**Performance:** maximum speed 30+kt
**Range:** 9,660km (6,000 miles) at 20kts
**Complement:** 33 + 327
**Ships:** 27; *Ticonderoga* (CG 47) + 26

*Below: PHILIPPINE SEA (CG 58) (Aldino)*

# VIRGINIA CLASS

**Type:** cruiser (CGN)
**Country:** United States of America
**Displacement:** 8,625 tons standard and 11,300 tons full load
**Dimensions:** length 178.4m (585ft); beam 19.2m (63ft); draught 9.6m (31.5ft)
**Gun armament:** two 127mm (5in)/54 Mk 45 Mod 0 and two GE/GD 20mm (0.79in) Vulcan Phalanx Mk 15
**Missile armament:** two quadruple container-launchers for eight McDonnell Douglas Harpoon SSMs, two Mk 26 twin launchers for a maximum of 50 GDC Standard SM-2MR SAMs and two quadruple launchers for eight GDC Tomahawk SLCM
**Anti-submarine armament:** two triple tube mountings for 324mm (12.75in) Mk 46 or Mk 50 A/S torpedoes, up to 20 Honeywell ASROC missiles
**Electronics:** air search; surface search; navigation radars; fire control; bow-mounted EDO/GE SQS 53A sonars, and electronic countermeasures
**Propulsion:** two pressurised water cooled General Electric D2G nuclear reactors supplying steam to two sets of geared turbines delivering 74,570kW (100,000shp) to two shafts
**Performance:** maximum speed 30kt
**Complement:** 27 + 445
**Ships:** two; *Mississippi* (CGN 40) *below centre, Arkansas* (CGN 41) *below front*

# DESTROYERS

Both battleships and cruisers have always been large ships, even in their pre-dreadnought era. During its lifetime, however, the destroyer metamorphosed from craft of less than 300 tons, through 1,000 tons at the time of the First World War, to about 2,500 tons for the Second World War; in some cases to as much as 8,000 tons in the period after the Cold War.

The type proliferated during both world wars, growing to symbolise the whole purpose of the navy more than any other vessel. However today it is only the USA that is planning to build any new destroyer classes, as the type is rapidly being replaced elsewhere by the advent of the frigate, which is now the most numerous combatant.

*Below:* Fletcher class destroyers of the Hellenic navy; left, E NAVARINON (D63) and right, ASPIS (D06). The Fletcher class was the US Navy's most important fleet destroyer class of the Second World War, having a full load displacement of 3,050 tons and a maximum speed of 32kt. It served with particular distinction in the Pacific theatre. Gun armament consisted of four 127mm (5in)/ 38 DP in four Mk 30 single mountings, six 76mm (3in)/55 DP in three Mk 33 twin mountings and ten 40mm (1.57in) Bofors AA in two single and two quadruple mountings. The type was retained in service after the war but released for export from the 1950s onwards

The modern destroyer's role is to provide area defence for the task force/ group against air attack. This defence is provided in the form of a triple layer, beginning with the directing of carrier-borne aircraft against enemy attack. This is backed up by the second layer, the craft's own SAMs, deployed against any enemy aircraft that have penetrated the first layer; and then by the final layer, the close-in weapons systems. This array of armament also enables the destroyer to engage in shore bombardment, while carrying a helicopter provides an anti-submarine and anti-surface vessel capability.

The vast majority of destroyers built after 1960 have been in the guided missile vessel category, the exceptions all having embarked helicopters for anti-submarine warfare deployment. The largest such class is the American Spruance class, which must be regarded as the most capable anti-submarine warfare ships ever built, but no large ASW class destroyers are known to have been built anywhere since the mid-1980s.

**Above:** US Navy Coontz class guided missile destroyer, KING (DDG41), was originally commissioned as a frigate, equipped with both SSMs and SAMs

Most countries embarked on a building programme of building guided missile destroyers during the late 1950s and early 1960s, America leading the way with the ten-ship Coontz class. These were laid down in 1957, began to enter service in 1961, and were followed by the smaller 23-vessel Charles F. Adams class, *illustrated above*, which entered service with the US Navy in 1964. They were built also for Australia and West Germany, and were purchased by Greece when retired from the US Navy in the 1990s.

US production was matched by the Soviet Union with its Krupny class, the first of which was laid down in 1958. Britain laid down the first of the very large County class destroyers in the following year.

France, Italy and the Netherlands built destroyers during the 1960s, with production being continued by most of the naval powers until the late 1980s, when costs were becoming a major factor, deterring any further wide-scale production. In Europe the last guided missile destroyers were the British Manchester class, the building of which ended in 1985, the French Cassard class, 1991, and the Italian Luigi Durand de la Penne class, 1993.

China also completed the single Luhu class in 1993 and more recently Japan has completed the fourth of its large Kongo Aegis class, leaving only America as the current builder of destroyers with its Arleigh Burke Aegis class ships.

**Above:** the US Navy's ELLIOTT (DD967) is one of the 31 ships of the Spruance class. Built to replace the Gearing class destroyers, they were the first large US warships to employ entirely gas turbine propulsion

An artist's impression of the United Kingdom's new Type 45 destroyer. The three ships will replace the existing Type 42 class. Provisional specifications include a displacement of 7,200 tons full load, a maximum speed of 29kt and a complement of approximately 190. The second ship is to be named HMS DAUNTLESS (Aldino)

# ALMIRANTE BROWN (MEKO 360H2) CLASS

**Type:** destroyer (DDG)
**Country:** Argentina
**Displacement:** 3,360 tons full load
**Dimensions:** length 125.9m (413ft); beam 14m (46ft); draught 5.8m (19ft)
**Gun armament:** one 127mm (5in)/54 DP OTO Melara; eight Breda/Bofors 40mm (1.57in)/70 guns
**Missile armament:** two quad Exocet SSM launchers; one octuple SAM launcher
**Aircraft:** two SA 3 19B Alouette III helicopters
**Electronics:** air/surface search; surface search; navigation; fire control and hull-mounted Atlas Elektronik 80 sonars
**Propulsion:** four gas turbines delivering to twin shafts
**Performance:** maximum speed 30.5kt
**Range:** 7,250km (4,500 miles) at 18kt
**Complement:** 200
**Ships:** four; *Almirante Brown* (D 10), *La Argentina* (D 11), *Heroina* (D 12), and *Sarandi* (D 13)

*Below:* the German-built ALMIRANTE BROWN, in the foreground, was launched in 1981. A similar vessel, built for Nigeria, is classified as a frigate

# PERTH CLASS

**Type:** destroyer (DDG)
**Country:** Australia
**Displacement:** 3,370 tons standard and 4,618 tons full load
**Dimensions:** length 134.3m (440.8ft); beam 14.3m (47.1ft); draught 6.1m (20.1ft)
**Gun armament:** two FMC 127mm (5in)/54 Mk 42 Mod 10; two GE/GD 20mm (0.79in) Mk 15 Vulcan Phalanx; up to six 12.7mm (0.5in) MGs
**Missile armament:** GDC Pomona Standard SM-1MR SAM launcher; dual capability Harpoon SSM launcher; two triple 324mm (12.75in) torpedo tubes for Honeywell Mk 46 Mod 5
**Aircraft:** none
**Electronics:** Hughes SPS 52C and Lockheed SPS 40C air search; Norden SPS 67V surface search; two Raytheon SPG 51C and Western Electric SPG 53F fire control systems and hull-mounted Sangamo SQS 23KL sonars
**Propulsion:** four Foster-Wheeler boilers supplying steam to two sets of General Electric double reduction geared turbines delivering 52,200kW (70,000shp) to two shafts
**Performance:** maximum speed 30+kt
**Range:** 9,660km (6,000 miles) at 15kt
**Complement:** 21 + 312
**Ships:** three; *Perth* (38), *Hobart* (39), and *Brisbane* (41)
**Remarks:** this Australian version of the highly successful Charles F. Adams class guided-missile destroyer forms the 1st Destroyer Squadron. The Australian ships differ relatively little from their American counterparts, the most significant modification being the wide deckhouse between the funnels for their original Ikara anti-submarine missile system, making them almost identical to the Greek Kimon class. The ships were laid down in 1962 (D 38 and D 39) and 1965 (D 41), commissioned in 1965 (D 38 and D 39) and 1967 (D 41). All ships were upgraded between 1974 and 1979, with a further modernisation from 1985 to add the Harpoon anti-ship missiles and the Mk 13 missile launcher. At the same time as this later upgrading was carried out, the Ikara ASW system was removed and all ships received the Phalanx CIWS, new search and fire-control radars, decoy and ECM equipment. Recognition features include a high bow with sweeping forecastle, a high bridge structure topped by a SATCOM dome, two funnels that slop aftwards and a tripod mainmast that straddles the forward funnel.

# IROQUOIS CLASS

**Type:** destroyer (DDG)
**Country:** Canada
**Displacement:** 3,550 tons standard and 5,100 tons full load
**Dimensions:** length 129.8m (426ft); beam 15.2m (50ft); draught 4.7m (15.5ft)
**Gun armament:** one 76mm (3in)/62 OTO Melara Super Rapid; one GE/GD 20mm (0.79in)/76 six-barrelled Vulcan Phalanx Mk 15
**Missile armament:** one Martin Marietta Mk 41 VLS SAM
**Torpedoes:** two triple 324mm (12.75in) Mk 32 tubes, Honeywell Mk 46 torpedoes
**Aircraft:** two Sikorsky CH-124 Sea King ASW helicopters
**Propulsion:** two Pratt & Whitney FT4A2 gas turbines delivering 37,285kW (50,000shp) gas turbines delivering 5,520kW (7,400shp) to two shafts
**Performance:** maximum speed 29+kt
**Range:** 7,250km (4,500 miles) at 20kt
**Complement:** 20 + 225
**Ships:** four; *Iroquois* (280) *illustrated below*, *Huron* (281), *Athabaskan* (282), and *Algonquin* (283)

# ALMIRANTE CLASS

**Type:** destroyer (DD)
**Country:** Chile
**Displacement:** 3,300 tons full load
**Dimensions:** length 122.6m (402ft); beam 13.1m (43ft) draught 4m (13.3ft)
**Gun armament:** four Vickers 102mm (4in)/60 Mk(N)R, four Bofors 40mm (1.57in)/70
**Missile armament:** four Aerospatiale MM 38 Exocet SSM; two Short Brothers Seacat quad launchers for SAMs
**Torpedoes:** two triple 324mm (12.75in) Mk 32 tubes, Honeywell Mk 44 Mod 1
**A/S mortars:** two 3 barrelled Admiralty Squid DC motors
**Electronics:** air-search; air/surface-search; navigation; gun fire-control radars; hull-mounted sonars
**Propulsion:** two boilers supplying steam to two sets of gas turbines delivering 40,270kW (54,000shp) to two shafts
**Performance:** maximum speed 34.5kt
**Range:** 5,925km (3,680 miles) at 16kt
**Complement:** 266
**Ships:** two, *Almirante Riveros* (18), and *Almirante Williams* (19)

*Below: ALMIRANTE RIVEROS is among the oldest destroyers still in service anywhere; both ships of the class were commissioned in 1960*

# PRAT (ex COUNTY) CLASS

**Type:** destroyer (DDG)
**Country:** Chile
**Displacement:** 6,200 tons full load
**Dimensions:** length 158.7m (520.5ft); beam 16.5m (54ft) draught 6.3m (20.5ft)
**Gun armament:** two Vickers 115mm (4.5in) Mk 6; two or four Oerlikon 20mm (0.79in) Mk 9; two Bofors 40mm (1.57in)/60 (*Latorre* only); 12.7mm (0.5in) single or twin MGs
**Missile armament:** four Aerospatiale MM 38 Exocet SSMs; Short Brothers Sea Slug Mk 2 and Israeli Barak I SAMs
**Torpedoes:** six 324mm (12.75in) Mk 32 tubes
**Electronics:** air-search; surface-search; navigation; gun fire-control radars and hull-mounted sonars
**Aircraft:** one Bell 206B or two NAS 332F Super Puma helicopters
**Propulsion:** four gas turbines, two geared steam turbines, two shafts
**Performance:** maximum speed 30kt
**Range:** 5,635km (3,500 miles) at 28kt
**Complement:** 470
**Ships:** four; *Prat* (11), ex *Norfolk*; *Cochrane* (12), ex *Antrim*; *Latorre* (14), ex *Glamorgan*, and *Blanco Encalada* (15), ex *Fife*

# LUDA (TYPE 051) CLASS

**Type:** destroyer (DDG)
**Country:** China
**Displacement:** 3,670 tons full load
**Dimensions:** length 132m (433.1ft); beam 12.8m (42ft) draught 4.6m (15ft)
**Gun armament:** four 130mm (5.1in)/58 DP, two 100mm (3.94in)/56 DP, six or eight 37mm (1.46in)/63 AA and eight 25mm (1in)/60 AA
**Missile armament:** six HY-2 SSM launchers; octuple SAM launcher
**Torpedoes:** six 324mm (12.75in) tubes
**Electronics:** air-search; navigation; gun fire-control radars, hull-mounted sonar
**Propulsion:** four boilers, two sets of geared turbines, two shafts
**Performance:** maximum speed 32kt
**Range:** 4,780km (2,970 miles) at 18kt or 2,000km (1,245 miles) at 32kt
**Complement:** 27 + 258
**Ships:** 17, *Jinan* (105) + 16

# LUHU CLASS

**Type:** destroyer (DDG)
**Country:** China
**Displacement:** 4,200 tons full load
**Dimensions:** length 145m (475.7ft); beam 15.2m (49.9ft) draught 5.1m (16.7ft)
**Gun armament:** two 100mm (3.94in)/56; eight 37mm (1.46in)/63
**Missile armament:** eight YJ-1 SSM launchers; one octuple SAM launcher
**Torpedoes:** six 324mm (12.75in) tubes
**Anti-submarine armament:** two FQF 2500 mortar launchers
**Electronics:** air-search; air/surface-search; gun fire-control radars and hull-mounted sonars
**Aircraft:** two Harbin Z9A (Dauphin) helicopters
**Performance:** maximum speed 30kt
**Ships:** one, *Haribing* (112), and one ordered

# CASSARD CLASS

**Type:** destroyer (DDG)
**Country:** France
**Displacement:** 4,730 tons full load
**Dimensions:** length 139m (455.9ft); beam 14m (45.9ft) draught 6.5m (21.3ft)
**Gun armament:** one 100mm (3.94in)/55 Mod 68 CADAM; two Oerlikon 20mm (0.79in); four 12.7mm (0.5in) MGs
**Missile armament:** eight Aerospatiale Exocet SSM launchers; SAM launchers
**Torpedoes:** two launchers
**Electronics:** air-search; air/surface-search; navigation; gun fire-control radars, and hull-mounted sonar
**Aircraft:** one Aerospatiale Panther (originally Lynx Mk 4) helicopter
**Propulsion:** four diesel engines delivering power to two shafts
**Performance:** maximum speed 29.5kt
**Range:** 13,200km (8,200 miles) at 17kt
**Complement:** 225
**Ships:** two; *Cassard* (D614), and *Jean Bart* (D615)
**Remarks:** both ships were launched in the 1980s, following both serious delays because of financial constraints and doubts about the effectiveness of the Standard SM-1 surface-to-air missile system which is now to be replaced when the ships are refitted

# GEORGES LEYGUES (TYPE F 70) CLASS

**Type:** destroyer (DDG)
**Country:** France
**Displacement:** 3,850 tons standard and 4,170 tons full load
**Dimensions:** length 139m (455.9ft); beam 14m (45.9ft); draught 5.7m (18.7ft)
**Gun armament:** one 100mm (3.94in)/55; two Oerlikon 20mm (0.79in)
**Missile armament:** four Aerospatiale MM 38 Exocet SSM launchers; one octuple launcher for Thomson-CFS Crotale SAMs
**Torpedoes:** two tubes for Honeywell Mk 46
**Aircraft:** two Westland Lynx Mk 4 helicopters
**Propulsion:** gas turbines delivering 38,775kW (52,000bhp) to two shafts
**Performance:** maximum speed 30kt on gas turbines or 21kt on diesels
**Range:** 13,685km (8,500 miles) at 18kt on diesels
**Complement:** 218
**Ships:** seven; *Georges Leygues* (D640) *illustrated opposite,* with Alouette III landing, *Dupleix* (D641), *Montcalm* (D642), *Jean de Vienne* (D643), *Primauguet* (D644), *La Motte-Picquet* (D645), and *Latouche-Tréville* (D646)

# SUFFREN CLASS

**Type:** destroyer (DDG)
**Country:** France
**Displacement:** 5,090 tons standard and 6,910 tons full load
**Dimensions:** length 157.6m (517.1ft); beam 15.5m (51ft); draught 6.1m (20ft)
**Gun armament:** two 100mm (3.94in)/55 DP; four Oerlikon 20mm (0.79in) AA
**Missile armament:** four MM 38 Exocet SSM launchers; twin Masurca SAM launcher
**Electronics:** air-search; air/surface-search; navigation; gun-control radar; hull-mounted active search and attack sonar
**Propulsion:** four boilers supplying steam to two sets of Rateau double-reduction geared turbines delivering 54,065kW (72,500shp) to two shafts
**Performance:** maximum speed 34kt
**Range:** 8,200km (5,100 miles) at 18kt or 4,450km (2,765 miles) at 29kt
**Complement:** 23 + 332
**Ships:** two; *Suffren* (D602) and *Duquesne* (D603). Designed to protect French carriers against air and submarine threat, both ships were laid down in the early 1960s, *Suffren* being commissioned in 1967 *Duquesne* in 1970

# TOURVILLE (TYPE F 67) CLASS

**Type:** destroyer (DDG)
**Country:** France
**Displacement:** 4,580 tons standard and 5,950 tons full load
**Dimensions:** length 152.8m (501.6ft); beam 16m (52.4ft); draught 5.7m (18.7ft)
**Gun armament:** two 100mm (3.94in)/55 DP; two 20mm (0.79in) AA
**Missile armament:** six Aerospatiale MM 38 Exocet SSM launchers; Thomson-CSF Crotale SAR launchers
**Anti-submarine armament:** one launcher for 13 Malafon L4 torpedoes; two launchers for 10 ECAN L5 torpedoes
**Aircraft:** one Lynx Mk 4 helicopter
**Electronics:** air search; air/surface-search; navigation; fire-control radars, and bow-mounted sonar
**Propulsion:** four boilers supplying steam to two sets of Rateau double-reduction geared turbines delivering 40,565kW (54,400shp) to two shafts
**Performance:** maximum speed 32kt
**Range:** 9,250km (5,750 miles) at 18kt or 3,500km (2,175 miles) at 30kt
**Complement:** 17 + 113 + 162
**Ships:** three; *Tourville* (D 610); *Duguay-Trouin* (D 611), *illustrated below*, and *De Grasse* (D 612)

# LÜTJENS (TYPE 103B) CLASS

**Type:** destroyer (DDG)
**Country:** Germany
**Displacement:** 3,950 tons standard and 4,560 tons full load
**Dimensions:** length 133.2m (437ft); beam 14.32m (47ft); draught 6.1m (20ft)
**Gun armament:** two FMC 127mm (5in)/54 DP Mk 42 Mod 10 automatic
**Missile armament:** Harpoon SSM launchers; Standard SM-1MR SAM launcher
**Anti-submarine armament:** Honeywell ASROC Mk 1 octuple launcher
**Electronics:** air-search; surface-search; fire-control radar systems and hull-mounted sonar
**Propulsion:** two turbines delivering to two shafts
**Performance:** maximum speed 32kt
**Range:** 7,250km (4,500 miles) at 20kt
**Complement:** 337
**Ships:** three; *Lütjens* (D 185), ex US Charles F. Adams class DDG 28; *Mölders* (D186), ex US Charles F. Adams class DDG 29, and *Rommel* (D 187), ex US Charles F. Adams class DDG 30

# AUDACE CLASS

**Type:** destroyer (DDG)
**Country:** Italy
**Displacement:** 4,400 tons full load
**Dimensions:** length 136.6m (448ft); beam 14.2m (46.6ft); draught 4.6m (15.1ft)
**Gun armament:** one 127mm (5in)/54 DP; three 76mm (3in)/62 DP
**Missile armament:** four twin SSM launchers; Standard SM-1 MR SAM launcher; octuple Selenia Albatros launcher for Aspide missiles
**Torpedoes:** six 324mm (12.75in) tubes for Honeywell Mk 46
**Aircraft:** two Agusta-Bell AB212 ASW helicopters
**Electronics:** long-range air-search; air search; air/surface search; surface search; navigation; fire-control radar systems and hull-mounted sonar
**Propulsion:** four Foster-Wheeler boilers supplying steam to two double-reduction geared turbines delivering 54,440kW (73,000shp) to two shafts
**Performance:** maximum speed 34kt
**Range:** 5,560km (3,455 miles) at 20kt
**Complement:** 30 + 350
**Ships:** two; *Ardito* (D 550), and *Audace* (D 551)

# DE LA PENNE (ex ANIMOSO) CLASS

**Type:** destroyer (DDG)
**Country:** Italy
**Displacement:** 5,400 tons full load
**Dimensions:** length 147.7m (487.4ft); beam 16.1m (52.8ft); draught 5m (16.5ft)
**Gun armament:** one OTO Melara 127mm (5in)/54 DP; three OTO Melara 76mm (3in)/62 DP Super Rapid
**Missile armament:** four or eight OTO Melara/Matra Teseo Mk 2 (TG 2) SSM launchers; GDC Pomona Standard SM-1 MR SAM launcher; octuple Selenia Albatros Mk 2 launcher for Aspide missiles
**Torpedoes:** two triple 324mm (12.75in) tubes for Whitehead A 290
**Aircraft:** two Agusta-Bell AB212 ASW helicopters
**Electronics:** long-range air-search; air search; air/surface search; surface search; navigation; fire-control radar systems and integrated hull sonar
**Performance:** maximum speed 31.5kt
**Range:** 11,270km (7,000 miles) at 18kt
**Ships:** two; *Luigi Durand De La Penne* (D 560), ex *Animoso*, and *Francesco Mimbelli* (D 561), ex *Ardimentoso*

*Below:* ANIMOSO, *photographed prior to her renaming, has a right aft flight deck with an open quarterdeck below*

# ASAGIRI CLASS

**Type:** destroyer (DDG)
**Country:** Japan
**Displacement:** 4,200 tons full load
**Dimensions:** length 137m (449.5ft); beam 14.6m (47.9ft); draught 4.45m (14.6ft)
**Gun armament:** one 76mm (3in) OTO Melara L/62 DP; two 20mm (0.79in) GE/GD Phalanx Mk 15 CIWS
**Missile armament:** eight McDonnell Douglas Harpoon SSM launchers; octople launcher for Sea Sparrow SAMs
**Torpedo armament:** six 324mm (12.75in) tubes for Honeywell Mk 46
**Anti-submarine armament:** octople launcher for Honeywell ASROC Mk 112
**Aircraft:** one Mitsubishi HSS-2B Sea King or SH-60J Sea Hawk helicopter
**Electronics:** air-search; surface-search; fire-control radar systems, and hull-mounted sonar
**Propulsion:** four gas turbines delivering 40,260kW (54,000shp) to two shafts
**Performance:** maximum speed 30+kt
**Complement:** 220
**Ships:** seven; *Asagiri* (DD 151), *illustrated below,* note that her main mast is offset to port – it is central in all other ships of the class; *Yamagiri* (DD 152); *Yuugiri* (DD 153); *Amagiri* (DD 154); *Hamagiri* (DD 155); *Setogiri* (DD 156); *Sawagiri* (DD 157), and *Umigiri* (DD 158)

# HARUNA CLASS

**Type:** destroyer (DDG)
**Country:** Japan
**Displacement:** 4,950 tons *Haruna,* 5,050 tons *Hiei* full load
**Dimensions:** length 153m (502ft); beam 17.5m (57.4ft); draught 5.2m (17.1ft)
**Gun armament:** two FMC 127mm (5in)/54 DP Mk 42 automatic; two GE/GD 20mm (0.79in) Phalanx Mk 15 CIWS
**Missile armament:** octuple launcher for Sea Sparrow SAMs
**Anti-submarine armament:** octuple launcher for Honeywell ASCOR Mk 112
**Aircraft:** three Mitsubishi HSS-2B Sea King helicopters
**Electronics:** air-search; surface-search; fire-control radar systems, and hull-mounted sonars
**Propulsion:** turbines delivering power to two shafts
**Performance:** maximum speed 31kt
**Range:** 8,894km (5,525 miles)
**Complement:** 370
**Ships:** two; *Haruna* (DD 141) and *Hiei* (DD 142)

*Below: HIEI, which, like her sister ship, was intended to serve as a command ship for anti-submarine escort groups. They are the only destroyers in the world to carry three large A/S helicopters*

# HATAKAZE CLASS

**Type:** destroyer (DDG)
**Country:** Japan
**Displacement:** 4,600 tons standard and 5,500 tons full load
**Dimensions:** length 150m (492.1ft); beam 16.4m (53.8ft); draught 4.7m (15.4ft)
**Gun armament:** two 127mm (5in)/54 DP; two 20mm (0.79in) Phalanx Mk 15
**Missile armament:** eight Harpoon SSM launchers; Standard SAM launcher
**Torpedoes:** six 324mm (12.75in) tubes for Honeywell Mk 46 Mod 5 Neartip
**Anti-submarine armament:** octuple launcher for Honeywell ASCOR Mk 112
**Aircraft:** one Mitsubishi HSS-3B Sea King or SH-60J Sea Hawk helicopter, on a platform aft
**Electronics:** air-search; surface-search; fire-control radar systems, and hull-mounted sonars
**Propulsion:** four gas turbines delivering power to two shafts
**Performance:** speed 32kt
**Complement:** 260
**Ships:** two, *Hatakaze* (DD 171) and *Shimakaze* (DD 172), *illustrated below*; like her sister ship, she features a long flight deck above an open quarterdeck

# HATSUYUKI (TYPE 122) CLASS

**Type:** destroyer (DDG)
**Country:** Japan
**Displacement:** 3,050 tons standard and 3,700 tons full load
**Dimensions:** length 130m (426.5ft); beam 13.6m (44.6ft); draught 4.2m (13.8ft)
**Gun armament:** one 76mm (3in)/62 DP; two 20mm (0.79in) Phalanx Mk 15
**Missile armament:** two quad McDonnell Douglas Harpoon SSM launchers; Raytheon Sea Sparrow Type 3 SAM launcher
**Torpedoes:** six 324mm (12.75in) tubes for Honeywell Mk 46 Mod 5 Neartip
**Anti-submarine armament:** octuple Honeywell ASROC Mk 112 launcher
**Aircraft:** one Mitsubishi HSS-3B Sea King helicopter
**Electronics:** air-search; surface-search; fire-control radar systems, and hull-mounted sonar
**Propulsion:** COGOG (COmbined Gas Or Gas turbine) arrangement, with two gas turbines delivering 33,550kW (45,000shp) to two shafts
**Performance:** speed 30kt
**Complement:** 195
**Ships:** 12; *Hatsuyuki* (DD 122) + 11. The above details apply to *Hatsuyuki*

# KONGO CLASS

**Type:** destroyer (DDG)
**Country:** Japan
**Displacement:** 9,485 tons full load
**Dimensions:** length 161m (528.2ft); beam 21m (68.9ft); draught 6.2m (20.3ft)
**Gun armament:** one OTO Melara 127mm (5in)/54 DP; two GE/GD 20mm (0.79in) Vulcan Phalanx Mk 15
**Missile armament:** two quad McDonnell Douglas Harpoon SSM launchers; Standard SM-2MR SAM launcher
**Torpedoes:** six 324mm (12.75in) tubes for Honeywell Mk 46 Mod 5 Neartip
**Anti-submarine armament:** vertical launch ASROC
**Electronics:** air-search; surface-search; navigation; fire-control radar systems, and hull-mounted sonar
**Performance:** maximum speed 30kt
**Range:** 7,250km (4,500 miles) at 20kt
**Ships:** two; *Kongo* (DD 173), *Kirishima* (DD 174) + two building

# MINEGUMO CLASS

**Type:** destroyer (DD)
**Country:** Japan
**Displacement:** 2,150 tons full load
**Dimensions:** length 114m (373.9ft); beam 11.8m (38.7ft); draught 4m (13.1ft)
**Gun armament:** four USN 76mm (3in)/50 DP in two Mk 33 twin mountings
**Torpedoes:** two triple 324mm (12.75in) Type 68 tubes
**Anti-submarine armament:** octuple launcher for Honeywell ASROC Mk 112
**Electronics:** air-search radar; surface-search; gun fire-control radar systems and one OQS-3 hull-mounted sonar
**Propulsion:** six Mitsubishi diesels delivering 19,760kW (26,500bhp) to two shafts
**Performance:** maximum speed 27kt
**Range:** 11,270km (7,000 miles) at 20kt
**Complement:** 210
**Ships:** three; *Minegumo* (DD 116), *Natsugumo* (DD 117), *Murakumo* (DD 118)

# MURASAME CLASS

**Type:** destroyer (DDG)
**Country:** Japan
**Displacement:** 5,100 tons full load
**Dimensions:** length 151m (494.4ft); beam 17.4m (57.1ft); draught 5.2m (17.1ft)
**Gun armament:** one 76mm (3in)/62 OTO Melara Compact; two GE/GD 20mm (0.79in) Vulcan Phalanx Mk 15
**Missile armament:** eight SSM-1B Harpoon launchers; Raytheon Mk 48 VLS Sparrow SAM launcher
**Torpedoes:** six 324mm (12.75in) Type 68 tubes
**Aircraft:** one SH-60J Sea Hawk helicopter
**Electronics:** air-search; surface-search; navigation; fire-control radar systems and hull-mounted Mitsubishi OQS-5 sonar
**Propulsion:** four gas turbines delivering power to two shafts
**Performance:** maximum speed 30kt
**Range:** 15,195km (9,438 miles) at 20kt
**Complement:** 166
**Ships:** four; *Murasame* (DD 101), *Harusame* (DD 102), *Yuudachi* (DD 103), *Kirisame* (DD 104) + five building

# SHIRANE CLASS

**Type:** destroyer (DDG)
**Country:** Japan
**Displacement:** 5,200 tons standard and 6,800 tons full load
**Dimensions:** length 159m (521.5ft); beam 17.5m (57.5ft); draught 5.3m (17.3ft)
**Gun armament:** two 127mm (5in)/54 DP Mk 42 automatic; two GE/GD 20mm (0.79in) Phalanx Mk 15 CIWS
**Missile armament:** octuple launcher for Raytheon Sea Sparrow Mk 29 SAM
**Anti-submarine armament:** Honeywell ASROC Mk 112 octuple launcher
**Torpedoes:** six 324mm (12.75in) Type 68 tubes for Honeywell Neartip
**Aircraft:** three SH-60J Sea Hawk helicopters
**Electronics:** air-search; surface-search; navigation; fire-control radar systems and hull-mounted and towed-array sonars
**Propulsion:** boilers supplying steam to two sets of geared turbines delivering 52,200kW (70,000shp) to two shafts
**Performance:** maximum speed 32kt
**Complement:** 350
**Ships:** two; *Shirane* (DD 143), and *Kurama* (DD 144)

*Below:* Tachikaze class guided missile destroyers
are a dual-role type with capability in the
anti-submarine and anti-aircraft roles.
SAWAKAZE is an improved version, also having
anti-ship capability bestowed in the
provision of two quadruple container
launchers for RGM-84 Harpoon SSMs

# TACHIKAZE CLASS

**Type:** destroyer (DDG)
**Country:** Japan
**Displacement:** 3,900 tons standard and 4,800 tons full load
**Dimensions:** length 143m (469.2ft); beam 14.3m (46.9ft); draught 4.6m (15ft)
**Gun armament:** two 127mm (5in)/l54 DP; two 20mm (0.79in) Phalanx Mk 15 CIWS mountings
**Missile armament:** eight McDonnell Douglas Harpoon SSM launchers; Standard SM-1MR SAM launcher
**Anti-submarine armament:** Honeywell ASROC Mk 112 octuple launcher
**Torpedoes:** two triple 324mm (12.75in) Type 68 tubes for Honeywell Neartip
**Electronics:** air-search; surface-search; fire-control radar systems, and hull-mounted sonar
**Propulsion:** two geared steam turbines delivering 44,740kW (60,000shp) to two shafts
**Performance:** maximum speed 32kt
**Range:** 12,970km (8,065 miles) at 20kt
**Complement:** 260
**Ships:** three, *Tachikaze* (DD 168), *Asakaze* (DD 169), *Sawakaze* (DD 170)

# SOVREMENNY CLASS

**Type:** destroyer (DDG)
**Country:** Russia and associated states
**Displacement:** 7,300 tons full load
**Dimensions:** length 156m (511.8ft); beam 17.3m (56.8ft); draught 6.5ft (21.3ft)
**Gun armament:** four 130mm (5.1in)/70 DP; four 30mm (1.18in) AA
**Missile armament:** two quad SS-N-22 SSM launchers; two SA-N-7 Gadfly SAM launchers
**Torpedo armament:** two twin 533mm (21in) tubes
**Anti-submarine armament:** two RBU 1000 six-barrel rocket launchers
**Aircraft:** one Kamov Ka-25 Hormone B or Ka-27 Helix helicopter
**Electronics:** air-search; surface-search; fire control systems radar and hull-mounted sonar
**Performance:** maximum speed 34kt
**Range:** 22,500km (14,000 miles) at 14kt
**Complement:** about 350
**Ships:** seventeen, *Sovremenny* + 16 + 3 building; *Otchyanny, illustrated below*

# UDALOY CLASS

**Type:** destroyer (DDG)
**Country:** Russia and associated states
**Displacement:** 8,700 tons full load
**Dimensions:** length 162m (531.5ft); beam 19.3m (63.3ft); draught 6.2m (20.3ft)
**Gun armament:** two 100mm (3.94in)/59 DP; four 30mm (1.18in)/65 AA
**Missile armament:** eight SS-N-9 Gauntlet SAM vertical launchers
**Torpedo armament:** two quadruple 533mm (21in) AS/ASW tubes
**Aircraft:** two Kamov Ka-27 Helix A helicopters
**Electronics:** air-search; surface-search; fire control radars; hull-mounted sonar
**Propulsion:** four gas turbines delivering power to two shafts
**Performance:** maximum speed 34kt
**Range:** 6,440km (4,000 miles) at 18kt
**Complement:** 300
**Ships:** eleven, *Udaloy* + 10

# GEARING (FRAM I) CLASS

**Type:** destroyer (DD)
**Country:** Taiwan
**Displacement:** 2,425 tons standard and 3,500 tons full load
**Dimensions:** length 119m (390.5ft); beam 12.6m (41.2ft); draught 5.8m (19ft)
**Gun armament:** one OTO Melara 76mm (3in)/62; one GE/GD 20mm (0.79in) Phalanx; two Bofors 40mm (1.57in)/70; four or six 12.7mm (0.5in) MGs
**Missile armament:** ten General Dynamics Standard SM 1-MR SAM launchers
**Anti-submarine armament:** Honeywell ASROC Mk 112 octuple launcher
**Torpedoes:** two triple 324mm (12.75in) US Mk 32 tubes
**Aircraft:** one McDonnell Douglas 500MD helicopter
**Electronics:** Signal DA-08 air-search; Raytheon SPS 10/SPS 58 surface-search; Signaal and Westinghouse fire control radars; hull-mounted Raytheon sonar
**Propulsion:** four boilers; two sets of geared steam turbines; two shafts
**Performance:** maximum speed 32.5kt
**Range:** 8,890km (5,525 miles) at 15kt
**Complement:** 331
**Ships:** seven, *Chien Yang* (912), ex USS *James E. Kyes* DD 787 + six

# TYPE 42 CLASS (BATCH 1 AND 2)

**Type:** destroyer (DDG)
**Country:** United Kingdom
**Displacement:** 4,100 tons full load
**Dimensions:** length 125m (412ft); beam 14.3m (47ft); draught 5.8m (19ft)
**Gun armament:** one 114mm (4.5in)/55 DP; four 20mm (0.79in); two GE/GD 20mm (0.79in) Vulcan Phalanx Mk 15
**Missile armament:** one twin launcher for Sea Dart SAMs
**Torpedoes:** two triple 324mm (12.75in) Plessey STWS Mk 3 tubes
**Aircraft:** one Westland Lynx HAS 3 helicopter
**Electronics:** air-search; surface-search; navigation; fire control radars; hull-mounted sonars
**Propulsion:** COGOG (COmbined Gas turbine Or Gas turbine) arrangement, with two Rolls-Royce Olympus TM3B gas turbines and two Rolls-Royce Tyne RM1A gas turbines driving two shafts
**Performance:** maximum speed 29kt
**Range:** 6,440km (4,000 miles) at 18kt
**Complement:** 312
**Ships:** four Batch 1, *Birmingham* (D 86), *inset right*; *Newcastle* (D 87); *Glasgow* (D 88); *Cardiff* (D 108); and four Batch 2, *Exeter* (D 89), *main illustration*; *Southampton* (D 90); *Nottingham* (D 91), and *Liverpool* (D 92)

# TYPE 42 CLASS (BATCH 3)

**Type:** destroyer (DDG)
**Country:** United Kingdom
**Displacement:** 4,675 tons full load
**Dimensions:** length 141.4m (462.8ft); beam 14.9m (49ft); draught 5.8m (19ft) to screws
**Gun armament:** one 114mm (4.5in)/55 DP Vickers Mk 8; two 20mm (0.79in) Oerlikon Mk 7A; two 20mm (0.79in) Oerlikon/BMARC; one or two GE/GD 20mm (0.79in) Vulcan Phalanx Mk 15
**Missile armament:** one twin launcher for Sea Dart SAMs
**Torpedoes:** two triple 324mm (12.75in) for Marconi Stingray
**Aircraft:** one Westland Lynx HAS 3 helicopter
**Propulsion:** gas turbines delivering to two shafts
**Performance:** maximum speed 30+kt
**Range:** 6,440km (4,000 miles) at 18kt
**Ships:** four; *Manchester* (D 95), *Gloucester* (D 96), *Edinburgh* (D 97), and *York* (D 98)

*Below: HMS Manchester, like her three sister ships, has an extremely long forecastle, some 15.25m (50ft) longer than the Batch 1 and 2 ships*

# ARLEIGH BURKE CLASS

**Type:** destroyer (DDG)
**Country:** United States of America
**Displacement:** 8,400 tons full load
**Dimensions:** length 153.8m (504.5ft); beam 20.4m (66.9ft); draught 9.1m (30ft)
**Gun armament:** one FMC 127mm (5in)/54 DP Mk 45 Mod 1 or 23; two GE/GD 20mm (0.79in) Vulcan Phalanx 6-barrelled Mk 15
**Missile armament:** eight McDonnell Douglas Harpoon and 56 GDC Tomahawk SLCM/SSMs in combination of land attack or anti-ship; GDC Standard SM-2MR Block 4 SAMs
**Torpedoes:** two triple 324mm (12.75in) Mk 32 Mod 14 tubes for Honeywell Mk 46 Mod 5
**Anti-submarine armament:** Honeywell ASROC; payload Mk 46 torpedoes; two Martin Marietta Mk 41 Vertical Launch Systems (VLS) for Tomahawk, standard and ASROC
**Electronics:** RCA SPY 1D, 3D air-search/fire control; Norden SPS 67(V)3 surface search; Raytheon SPS 64(V)9 navigation; 3 Raytheon/RCA SPG 62 fire-control radars, and Gould/Raytheon/GE SQQ 89(V)6 hull-mounted sonars
**Propulsion:** gas turbines delivering to two shafts
**Performance:** maximum speed 32kt
**Range:** 7,084km (4,400 miles) at 20kt
**Complement:** 303
**Ships:** five; *Arleigh Burke* (DDG 51); *Barry* (DDG 52), ex *John Barry*); *John Paul Jones* (DDG 53); *Curtis Wilbur* (DDG 54), and *Stout* (DDG 55). A further twelve are being built and a further five are proposed
**Remarks:** the Arleigh Burke class of guided missile destroyers was planned to replace the ageing Coontz class guided missile destroyers, Leahy class guided missile cruisers and Belknap class guided missile cruisers. The first in the class was launched in September 1989 with a design more akin to a cruiser in size and basic capability. The principal mission of the Arleigh Burke class is to provide effective anti-aircraft cover, for which it has the SPY 1D version of the Aegis area defence system. The ships are built entirely of steel with the exception of their aluminium funnels, and their vital areas are protected by some 130 tons of plastic Kevlar armour. They are the first US warships to be built fully-equipped for warfare in a nuclear, chemical or biological environment, the crew being confined in a citadel located within the hull and superstructure

# **KIDD** CLASS

**Type:** destroyer (DDG)
**Country:** United States of America
**Displacement:** 6,950 tons light and 9,574 tons full load
**Dimensions:** length 171.8m (563.3ft); beam 16.8m (55ft); draught 9.1m (30ft)
**Gun armament:** two 127mm (5in)/54 DP; two 20mm (0.79in) Vulcan
Phalanx Mk 15; four 12.7mm (0.5in) MGs
**Missile armament:** two quad McDonnell Douglas Harpoon SSM launchers
and 52 GDC Standard SM-2 MR SAMs
**Torpedoes:** two triple 324mm (12.75in) Mk 32 tubes for Honeywell
Mk 46 torpedoes
**Aircraft:** two Kaman SH-2F or one Sikorsky SH-60B helicopter
**Electronics:** air search; surface-search; navigation; fire-control radar
systems, bow-mounted sonar
**Propulsion:** four General Electric LM 2500 gas turbines delivering
59,655kW (80,000shp) to two shafts
**Performance:** maximum speed 33kt
**Range:** 12,880km (8,000 miles) at 17kt
**Complement:** 368
**Ships:** four; *Kidd* (DDG 993), *Callaghan* (DDG 994), *illustrated below*, *Scott*
(DDG 995), and *Chandler* (DDG 996)

# SPRUANCE CLASS

**Type:** destroyer (DD)
**Country:** United States of America
**Displacement:** 5,830 tons standard and 8,040 tons full load
**Dimensions:** length 171.7m (563.2ft); beam 16.8m (55.1ft); draught 8.8m (29ft) to sonar dome
**Gun armament:** two FMC 127mm (5in)/54 DP Mk 45 Mod 0; two GE/GD 20mm (0.79in) six-barrelled Mk 15 Vulcan Phalanx; four 12.7mm (0.5in) MGs
**Missile armament:** two quad McDonnell Douglas Harpoon SSM launchers; GDC Tomahawk SLCM; octuple Raytheon GMLS Mk 29 SAM launcher
**Torpedoes:** two triple 324mm (12.75in) Mk 32 tubes for Honeywell Mk 46 torpedoes
**Aircraft:** one Sikorsky SH-60B Seahawk or SH-2F Seasprite helicopter
**Electronics:** air search; surface-search; navigation; fire-control radar systems, bow-mounted sonar
**Propulsion:** four gas turbines delivering power to two shafts
**Performance:** maximum speed 33kt
**Range:** 9,660km (6,000 miles) at 20kt
**Complement:** 322
**Ships:** 31; *Spruance* (DD 963) + 30, including DD 983 *John Rogers, illustrated below* (Aldino)

# FRIGATES

Today the frigate is widely regarded as the general-purpose ship of the fleet, and as the smallest unit that can be deployed independently on a worldwide basis to carry out a variety of low-level deterrent tasks.

Frigates have now replaced destroyers as the most numerous combatants in most of the world's navies, although not all of the frigates still under commission would be capable of surviving in a modern war environment. Nonetheless the frigate has been a great ambassador in recent years, and represents a presence rather than an active fighting resource.

*Below:* ships of the Canadian Armed Forces on patrol, with the anti-submarine frigate HMCS ANNAPOLIS (DDH 265) left, PROTECTOR (AOR 509) centre, and a DDH 280 class destroyer right. ANNAPOLIS was originally commissioned in 1964 but in 1982 her active life was extended under the Destroyer Life Extension Programme

Frigates traditionally have been smaller than destroyers, and immediately after the Second World War the Admiralty re-classified most of its escort vessels as frigates, deploying them to show the flag in most theatres from 1945 onwards. Since then the category has been developed into more specialised roles and gained immeasurably in its importance.

The Royal Navy fully converted the Hunt class destroyers to fast anti-submarine frigates in the 1950s, in order to counter the threat from the rapidly-growing Soviet submarine fleet. These were followed by its first specialist frigates, the Whitby class, completed between 1956–58. By the end of that decade, specialist frigates armed with 114mm (4.5in) guns were being designed and built for anti-aircraft duties, and for aircraft direction. Since then, the Royal Navy had operated with the most famous class of post-war frigates, the Leanders, until 1993.

The Knox class of anti-submarine and anti-ship guided missile escort frigates, commissioned between 1971 and 1974, was the largest single warship class produced in the West between the end of the Second World War and the Oliver Hazard Perry class of 51 vessels, commissioned between 1977 and 1989. Both of these classes were produced in the USA.

The Knox class was designed to provide the US Navy with a second-line anti-submarine force of ocean-going capability for the escort of convoys and amphibious forces. Modelled on the preceeding Garcia and Brooke classes, its hull is enlarged to accommodate non-pressure-fired boilers.

Today most smaller navies opt for missile-armed small light frigates. Russia generally classifies these ships as patrol ships or small ASW ships, and has specialised in this type of craft. The former Soviet Union has offered them for sale on the international market since the end of the Cold War, with equipment that is very adequate for those nations eager to secure naval superiority in their particular spheres of influence.

The more capable frigates are those with embarked helicopters; since first the battleship and then the cruiser have disappeared, eventually to be followed by the destroyer, their continued role on the high seas seems almost assured.

*Right: BREMEN (F 207), leader of the class of the German navy's Type 122 guided missile frigates, was designed to replace its aging classes of destroyers and Köln class frigates. The Bremen class was developed from the Dutch Kortenaer class to meet the German navy's very specific requirements for a frigate able of operating in high-threat areas as an effective anti-ship and anti-submarine system.*

*The class was commissioned between April 1982 and October 1984; the BREMEN and her five sister ships were laid down between July 1979 and May 1981*

# MOURAD RAIS CLASS

**Type:** frigate (FFG)
**Country:** Algeria
**Displacement:** 1,900 tons full load
**Dimensions:** length 96.4m (316.3ft); beam 12.6m (41.3ft); draught 3.5m (11.5ft)
**Gun armament:** two twin 76mm (3in)/60 DP; two twin 30mm (1.18in)/65 DP
**Missile armament:** SA-N-4 Gecko twin SAM launcher
**A/S mortars:** two 12-barrelled RBU 6000
**Depth charges:** two racks
**Electronics:** air/surface-search; navigation; fire-control radar systems, hull-mounted sonar
**Propulsion:** two gas and one diesel turbines delivering power to three shafts
**Performance:** maximum speed 27kt (gas), 22kt (diesel)
**Range:** 2,900km (1,800 miles) at 14kt
**Complement:** 130
**Ships:** three, all Russian-built; *Mourad Rais* (901), *Rais Kellick* (902), and *Rais Korfou* (903)

# ESPORA (MEKO 140A) CLASS

**Type:** frigate (FFH)
**Country:** Argentina
**Displacement:** 1,700 tons full load
**Dimensions:** length 91.2m (299.1ft); beam 11.1m (36.4ft); draught 3.4m (11.2ft)
**Gun armament:** one OTO Melara 76mm (3in)/62 compact; two twin Breda 40mm (1.57in)/70; two 12.7mm (0.5in) MGs
**Missile armament:** four Aerospatiale MM 38 Exocet SSM launchers
**Torpedoes:** two triple 324mm (12.75in) ILAS tubes
**Aircraft:** one SA 319B Alouette III helicopter
**Electronics:** air/surface-search; navigation; fire-control radar systems, hull-mounted Atlas Elektronik ASQ 4 sonar
**Propulsion:** two diesel turbines delivering power to two shafts
**Performance:** maximum speed 27kt
**Range:** 6,440km (4,000 miles) at 18kt
**Complement:** 93
**Ships:** six; *Espora* (41), *Rosales* (42), *Spiro* (43), *Parker* (44), *Robinson* (45), and *Gomez Roca* (46)

# ADELAIDE CLASS

**Type:** frigate (FFG)
**Country:** Australia
**Displacement:** 4,100 tons full load
**Dimensions:** length 138.1m (453ft); beam 13.7m (45ft); draught 7.5m (24.5ft)
**Gun armament:** one OTO Melara 76mm (3in)/62 compact Mk 75; one GE/GD 20mm (0.79in) Mk 15 Vulcan Phalanx; up to six 12.7mm (0.5in) MGs
**Missile armament:** eight McDonnell Douglas Harpoon SSM launchers; GDC Pomona Standard SM-1MR SAM launcher
**Torpedoes:** two triple 324mm (12.75in) Mk 32 tubes for Honeywell Mk 46
**Aircraft:** two Sikorsky S-70B Seahawk helicopters or one Seahawk and one Squirrel
**Electronics:** air search; surface search/navigation; fire-control radar systems, hull-mounted sonar
**Propulsion:** two gas turbines delivering power to a single shaft
**Performance:** maximum speed 27kt (gas), 22kt (diesel)
**Range:** 7,250km (4,500 miles) at 20kt
**Complement:** 184
**Ships:** six; *Adelaide* (01), *Canberra* (02), *Sydney* (03), *Darwin* (04), *Melbourne* (05), and *Newcastle* (06)

# LEOPARD (TYPE 41) CLASS

**Type:** frigate (FF)
**Country:** Bangladesh
**Displacement:** 2,520 tons full load
**Dimensions:** length 103.6m (339.8ft); beam 12.2m (40ft); draught 4.7m (15.5ft)
**Gun armament:** two twin Vickers 115mm (4.5in)/45 Mk 6; one Bofors 40mm (1.57in)/60
**Missile armament:** none
**Torpedoes:** none
**Electronics:** Marconi Type 965 air search with single AKE 1 array; Plessey Type 993 air/surface search; Decca Type 978 and Kelvin Hughes Type 1007 navigation; Type 275 fire-control radar systems
**Performance:** maximum speed 24kt
**Range:** 12,075km (7,500 miles) at 16kt
**Ships:** two; *Abu Bakr* (F 15), ex HMS *Lynx*, and *Ali Haider* (F 17), ex HMS *Jaguar*

# SALISBURY (TYPE 41) CLASS

**Type:** frigate (FF)
**Country:** Bangladesh
**Displacement:** 2,408 tons full load
**Dimensions:** length 103.6m (339.8ft); beam 12.2m (40ft); draught 4.7m (15.5ft)
**Gun armament:** one twin Vickers 115mm (4.5in)/45 Mk 6; two Bofors 40mm (1.57in)/60
**Anti-submarine armament:** one triple-barrelled Squid Mk 4 mortars
**Electronics:** air search; air/surface search radars, height finder; surface search; navigation; fire control radars, and hull-mounted sonars
**Propulsion:** eight diesel engines supplying power to two shafts
**Performance:** maximum speed 24kt
**Range:** 12,075km (7,500 miles) at 16kt
**Complement:** 207
**Ships:** one; *Umar Farooq* (F 16), ex HMS *Llandaff*

*Below: the Belgian Navy's Wielingen class frigate* WESTDIEP

# WIELINGEN CLASS

**Type:** frigate (FFG)
**Country:** Belgium
**Displacement:** 2,430 tons full load
**Dimensions:** length 106.4m (349ft); beam 12.3m (40.3ft); draught 5.6m (18.4ft)
**Gun armament:** one 100mm (3.94in)/55 DP Creusot Loire Mod 68
**Missile armament:** two twin Aerospatiale MM 38 Exocet SSM launchers; octople Raytheon Sea Sparrow Mk 29 SAM launcher
**Torpedo armament:** two 533mm (21in) launchers for ECAN L5 Mod 4 torpedoes
**Anti-submarine armament:** one 375mm (14.76in) six-barrel rocket launcher
**Electronics:** air/surface search; surface search/fire control; navigation radars, and hull-mounted sonar
**Propulsion:** one gas turbine and two diesels delivering power to two shafts
**Performance:** maximum speed 26kt
**Range:** 9,660km (6,000 miles) at 15kt
**Complement:** 159
**Ships:** three; *Wielingen* (F 910), *Westdiep* (F 911), and *Wandelaar* (F 912)

# INHAÚMA CLASS

**Type:** frigate (FFH)
**Country:** Brazil
**Displacement:** 1,970 tons full load
**Dimensions:** length 95.83m (314ft); beam 11.4m (37.4ft); draught 3.7m (12.1ft)
**Gun armament:** one Vickers 115mm (4.5in) Mk 8; two Bofors 40mm (1.57in)/70
**Missile armament:** four Aerospatiale MM 40 Exocet SSMs
**Torpedoes:** two triple 324mm (12.75in) tubes for Honeywell Mk 46 Mod 5
**Aircraft:** one Westland Lynx helicopter
**Electronics:** surface search; navigation; fire control radars, and hull-mounted Atlas Elektronik DSQS 21C sonar
**Propulsion:** two diesel and one gas turbine delivering power to two shafts
**Performance:** maximum speed 27kt
**Range:** 6,440km (4,000 miles) at 15kt
**Complement:** 122
**Ships:** four; *Inhaúma* (V 30), *Jaceguay* (V 31), *Julio de Noronha* (V 32), and *Frontin* (V 33)

# NITEROI CLASS

**Type:** frigate (FFG)
**Country:** Brazil
**Displacement:** 3,707 tons full load
**Dimensions:** length 129.2m (424ft); beam 13.5m (44.2ft); draught 5.5m (18.2ft)
**Gun armament:** two Vickers 114mm (4.5in)/55; two Bofors 40mm (1.57in)/70
**Missile armament:** two twin Aerospatiale MM 40 Exocet SSM launchers; two triple Short Bros Seacat SAM launchers
**Anti-submarine armament:** one Ikara launcher for Honeywell Mk 46 torpedoes
**Aircraft:** one Westland Lynx SAH-11helicopter
**Electronics:** Plessey AWS 2 air/surface search; Signaal ZW 06 surface search; two Selenia Orion RTN 10X fire control radars, and hull-mounted sonar
**Propulsion:** four diesels, two gas turbines delivering power to two shafts
**Performance:** maximum speed 30kt
**Range:** 8,533km (5,300 miles) at 17kt
**Complement:** 217
**Ships:** six; *Niteroi* (F 40), *Defensora* (F 41), *Constitui ão* (F 42), *Liberal* (F 43) *Independ ncia* (F 44), *União* (F 45)

# PARÁ CLASS

**Type:** frigate (FFH)
**Country:** Brazil
**Displacement:** 3,403 tons full load
**Dimensions:** length 126.3m (414.5ft); beam 13.5m (44.2ft); draught 4.4m (14.5ft)
**Gun armament:** two USN 127mm (5in)/38 Mk 30
**Anti-submarine armament:** Honeywell ASROC Mk 112 octuple launcher
**Torpedoes:** two triple 324mm (12.75in) tubes
**Aircraft:** one Westland Lynx SAH-11 helicopter
**Electronics:** air search; surface search; navigation; fire control radars, and bow-mounted EDO/General Electric SQS 26 AXR sonar
**Propulsion:** two boilers supplying steam to one geared turbine; single shaft
**Performance:** maximum speed 27.5kt
**Range:** 6,440km (4,000 miles) at 20kt
**Complement:** 239
**Ships:** four (ex US Garcia class); *Pará* (D 27), ex *Albert David*; *Paraíba* (D 28), ex *Davidson*; *Paraná* (VD 29), ex *Sample*, and *Pernambuco* (D 30), ex *Bradley*

*Below: the Niteroi class ship* CONSTITUI ÃO, *built by Vosper Thorneycroft*

# ANNAPOLIS CLASS

**Type:** frigate (FFH)
**Country:** Canada
**Displacement:** 2,930 tons full load
**Dimensions:** length 113.1m (371ft); beam 12.8m (42ft); draught 4.4m (14.5ft)
**Gun armament:** twin FMC 76mm (3in)/50 Mk 33
**Torpedoes:** two triple 324mm (12.75in) tubes for Honeywell Mk 46 Mod 5
**Aircraft:** one CH-124A Sea King ASW helicopter
**Electronics:** air/surface search; surface search; fire control radars, and hull-mounted sonars
**Propulsion:** two boilers supplying steam to geared turbines; two shafts
**Performance:** maximum speed 28kt
**Range:** 7,357km (4,570 miles) at 14kt
**Complement:** 246
**Ships:** two; *Annapolis* (265) and *Nipigon* (266)

*Below: ANNAPOLIS sails into Toronto harbour during a Great Lakes cruise. Under the Destroyer Life Extension Programme, Sea Sparrow SAMs, new air-search radar, new sonar and new electronic warfare systems were added during the period 1982–84*

# IMPROVED RESTIGOUCHE CLASS

**Type:** frigate (FF)
**Country:** Canada
**Displacement:** 2,390 tons standard and 2,900 tons full load
**Dimensions::** length 113.1m (371ft); beam 12.8m (42ft); draught 4.3m (14.1ft)
**Gun armament:** twin Vickers 76mm (3in)/70 Mk 30; one GE/GD 20mm (0.79in)/76 six-barrelled Vulcan Phalanx Mk 15; two Bofors 40mm (1.57in)/60
**Missile armament:** two quad McDonnell Douglas Harpoon launchers
**Anti-submarine armament:** Honeywell ASROC Mk 112 octuple launcher
**Torpedoes:** two triple 324mm (12.75in) tubes
**Electronics:** air search; surface search; navigation; fire control radars, and combined VDS and hull-mounted sonar
**Propulsion:** two boilers supplying steam to one geared turbine; single shaft
**Performance:** maximum speed 28kt
**Range:** 7,647km (4,750 miles) at 14kt
**Complement:** 214
**Ships:** four; *Gatineau* (236), *Restigouche* (257), *Kootenay* (258), and *Terra Nova* (259)

*Below:* HMCS R*ESTIGOUCHE* underway off Canada's west coast

# HALIFAX CLASS

**Type:** frigate (FFG)
**Country:** Canada
**Displacement:** 4,770 tons full load
**Dimensions:** length 134.7m (441.9ft); beam 16.4m (53.8ft); draught 4.9m (16.1ft)
**Gun armament:** one Bofors 57mm (2.24in)/70 Mk 2; one GE/GD 20mm (0.79in) Vulcan Phalanx Mk 15 Mod 1; eight 12.7mm (0.5in) MGs
**Missile armament:** two quad McDonnell Douglas Harpoon SSM launchers; two Raytheon Sea Sparrow Mk 48 octuple vertical launchers
**Torpedoes:** two twin 324mm (12.75in) tubes for Honeywell Mk 46 torpedoes
**Aircraft:** one CH-124A ASW or one CH-124B Heltas Sea King helicopter
**Electronics:** air search; air/surface-search; navigation; fire-control radar systems, hull-mounted Westinghouse SQS 505(V)6 sonar
**Propulsion:** two gas and one diesel turbines delivering power to two shafts
**Performance:** maximum speed 29kt
**Range:** 11,431km (7,100 miles) at 15kt
**Complement:** 198
**Ships:** eight; *Halifax* (330), *Vancouver* (331) + six, and four being built

# JIANGHU I CLASS

**Type:** frigate (FFH)
**Country:** China
**Displacement:** 1,702 tons full load
**Dimensions:** length 103.2m (338.5ft); beam 10.8m (35.4ft); draught 3.1m (10.2ft)
**Gun armament:** two twin China 100mm (3.94in)/56; one Creusot Loire 100mm (3.94in)/55; six twin China 37mm (1.46in)/63
**Missile armament:** two twin HY-2 (C-201) SSM launchers
**Torpedoes:** two triple 324mm (12.75in) ILAS tubes
**Aircraft:** one Harbin Z-9A (Dauphin) helicopter
**Electronics:** air/surface search; surface search/fire-control; navigation; fire-control radar systems, hull-mounted Echo Type 5 sonar
**Propulsion:** two  diesels delivering power to two shafts
**Performance:** maximum speed 30kt
**Range:** 6,440km (4,000 miles) at 15kt
**Complement:** 195
**Ships:** twenty-five, *Chang de* (509) + 24

# JIANGHU III AND IV CLASS

**Type:** frigate (FF)
**Country:** China
**Displacement:** 1,924 tons full load
**Dimensions:** length 103.2m (338.5ft); beam 10.8m (35.4ft); draught 3.1m (10.2ft)
**Gun armament:** two twin China 100mm (3.94in)/56; four twin China 37mm (1.46in)/63
**Missile armament:** eight YJ-1 (Eagle Strike) (C-801) SSM launchers
**Anti-submarine armament:** two RBU 1200 five-tubed mortar launchers
**Electronics:** air/surface search; surface search/fire-control; navigation; fire-control radar systems, Echo Type 5 hull-mounted sonar
**Propulsion:** two diesels delivering power to two shafts
**Performance:** maximum speed 26kt
**Range:** 6,440km (4,000 miles) at 15kt
**Complement:** 200
**Ships:** three; *Huangshi* (535), *Wu Hu* (536), *Zhoushan* (537), and one building

# JIANGWEI CLASS

**Type:** frigate (FFG)
**Country:** China
**Displacement:** 2,180 tons full load
**Dimensions:** length 112m (367.5ft); beam 12.4m (40.7ft); draught 4.3m (14.1ft)
**Gun armament:** twin China 100mm (3.94in)/56; four twin China 37mm (1.46in)/63
**Missile armament:** two triple YJ-1 (Eagle Strike) (C-801) SSM launchers; one HQ-61 sextuple SAM launcher
**Anti-submarine armament:** two RBU 1200 five-tubed mortar launchers
**Aircraft:** one Harbin Z-9A (Dauphin) helicopter
**Electronics:** Rice Screen air/surface search; Sun Visor and two Rice Lamp fire-control; Fin Curve navigation radar systems, Echo Type 5 hull-mounted sonar
**Propulsion:** two diesels delivering power to a two shafts
**Performance:** maximum speed 25kt
**Range:** 6,440km (4,000 miles) at 18kt
**Complement:** 170
**Ships:** four; *Anqing* (539), *Huainan* (540), *Huabei* (541), *Tongling* (542) and one building

# **ALMIRANTE PADILLA** CLASS

**Type:** frigate (FFH)
**Country:** Colombia
**Displacement:** 2,100 tons full load
**Dimensions:** length 99.1m (325.1ft); beam 11.3m (37.1ft); draught 3.7m (12.1ft)
**Gun armament:** one OTO Melara 76mm (3in)/62 compact; twin Breda 40mm (1.57in)/70; two twin Oerlikon 30mm (1.18in)/75 Mk 74
**Missile armament:** eight Aerospatiale MM 40 Exocet SSM launchers
**Torpedoes:** two triple 324mm (12.75in) Mk 32 tubes
**Aircraft:** one MBB BO 105 CB ASW helicopter
**Electronics:** Thomson-CFS Sea Tiger combined search; Castor II B fire-control radar systems, hull-mounted Atlas Elektronik ASO 4-2 active attack sonar
**Propulsion:** four diesels delivering power to two shafts
**Performance:** maximum speed 27kt
**Range:** 11,270km (7,000 miles) at 14kt
**Complement:** 94
**Ships:** four; *Almirante Padilla* (CM 51), *Caldas* (CM 52), *Antioquia* (CM 53), and *Independiente* (CM 54)

*Below: launched in 1982, the ALMIRANTE PADILLA, along with her sister ships, is overdue for a refit that would add surface-to-air missiles as a top priority*

# MODIFIED HVIDBJØREN CLASS

**Type:** frigate (FFH)
**Country:** Denmark
**Displacement:** 1,970 tons full load
**Dimensions:** length 74.7m (245ft); beam 12.2m (40ft); draught 5.3m (17.4ft)
**Gun armament:** one USN 76mm (3in)/50
**Missile armament:** none
**Torpedoes:** none
**Aircraft:** one Westland Lynx Mk 91 helicopter in a hanger aft
**Electronics:** Plessey AWS 6 air/surface search; Burmeister & Wain Elektronik Scanter Mil 009 navigation radar systems, hull-mounted Plessey PMS 26 sonar
**Propulsion:** three Burmeister & Wain Alpha diesels delivering 5,550kW (7,440bhp) to a single shaft
**Performance:** maximum speed 18kt
**Range:** 11,125km (6,195 miles) at 13kt
**Complement:** 59
**Ships:** one, *Beskytteren* (F 340)

*Below: like VAEDDEREN (F349), originally a Hvidbjøren class vessel and now re-classed as a Thetis class (F360), the sole ship of the Hvidbjøren Modified class is more an offshore patrol and fishery protection craft than a true warship*

# NIELS JUEL CLASS

**Type:** frigate (FFG)
**Country:** Denmark
**Displacement:** 1,320 tons full load
**Dimensions:** length 84m (275.5ft); beam 10.3m (33.8ft); draught 3.1m (10.2ft)
**Gun armament:** one OTO Melara 76mm (3in)/62 compact; four Oerlikon 20mm (0.79in)
**Missile armament:** two quad McDonnell Douglas Harpoon SSM launchers; octuple Raytheon NATO Sea Sparrow Mk 29 SAM launcher
**Electronics:** Plessey AWS 5, 3D air search; Philips 9GR 600 surface search; Burmeister & Wain Elektronik Scanter Mil 009 navigation; two Mk 95 and Philips 9LV 200 fire-control radar systems, hull-mounted Plessey PMS 26 sonar
**Propulsion:** one gas turbine, one diesel delivering power to two shafts
**Performance:** maximum speed 28kt
**Range:** 4,021km (2,500 miles) at 18kt
**Complement:** 94
**Ships:** three; *Niels Juel* (F 354), *Olfert Fischer* (F 355), and *Peter Tordenskiold* (F 356)

# THETIS CLASS

**Type:** frigate (FFH)
**Country:** Denmark
**Displacement:** 3,500 tons full load
**Dimensions:** length 112.5m (369.1ft); beam 14.4m (47.2ft); draught 6m (19.7ft)
**Gun armament:** one 76mm (3in) OTO Melara/62 Super Rapid; one or two 20mm (0.79in) Oerlikon
**Aircraft:** one Westland Lynx Mk 91 helicopter
**Electronics:** Plessey AWS 6 air/surface search; Terma Scanter Mil surface search; Furuno FR1505DA navigation; Bofors Electronic 9LV 200 fire-control radar systems, and Thomson Sintra TSM 2640 Salmon hull-mounted sonar and VDS
**Propulsion:** three diesel engines delivering power to a single shaft
**Performance:** maximum speed 20kt
**Range:** 13,685km (8,500 miles) at 18kt
**Complement:** 60
**Ships:** four; *Thetis* (F 357), *Triton* (F 358), *Vaedderen* (F 359), *Hvidbjøren* (F 360)

# D'ESTIENNE D'ORVES CLASS

**Type:** frigate (FF)
**Country:** France
**Displacement:** 1,250 tons full load
**Dimensions:** length 80m (262.5ft); beam 10.3m (33.8ft); draught 5.5m (18ft) to sonar dome and 3m (9.8ft) to keel
**Missile armament:** four Aerospatiale MM 40 Exocet SSM launchers
**Gun armament:** one DCN 100mm (3.94in)/55 Mod 68 CADAM; two Oerlikon 20mm (0.79in)
**Anti-submarine armament:** one sextuple 375mm (14.76in) rocket launcher
**Torpedoes:** four ECAN L5 tubes for 550mm (21.65in) L3 torpedoes
**Electronics:** air/surface search; navigation; fire-control radar systems, hull-mounted Thomson Sintra DUBA 25 sonar
**Propulsion:** twin screw diesel engines
**Performance:** maximum speed 23kt
**Range:** 7,245km (4,500 miles) at 15kt
**Complement:** 105
**Ships:** seventeen; *D'Estienne d'Orves* (F 781) + 16

*Below:* COMMANDANT DUCUING *(F 795), a D'Estienne d'Orves class frigate that entered service in the mid-1970s, designed for coastal ASW*

# FLORÉAL CLASS

**Type:** frigate (FFH)
**Country:** France
**Displacement:** 2,950 tons full load
**Dimensions:** length 93.6m (306.8ft); beam 14m (45.9ft); draught 4.3m (14.1ft)
**Gun armament:** one DNC 100mm (3.94in)/55 Mod 68 CADAM; two Giat 20 F2 20mm (0.79in)
**Missile armament:** two Aerospatiale MM 38 Exocet SSM launchers
**Aircraft:** one Dauphin II/Panther or Alouette III or one AS 332F Super Puma helicopter
**Electronics:** Thomson-CSF Mars DRBV 21A air/surface search; two Racal Decca DRBN 34A (1226) navigation radar systems
**Propulsion:** four diesel engines delivering power to two shafts

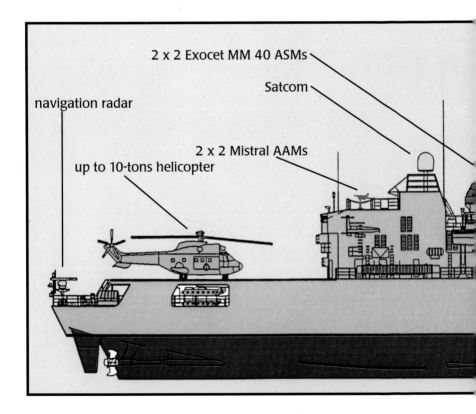

**Performance:** maximum speed 20kt
**Range:** 16,100km (10,000 miles) at 15kt
**Complement:** 86
**Ships:** six; *Floréal* (F 730), *Prairial* (F 731), *Niv se* (F 732), *Vent se* (F 733), *Vendémiaire* (F 734), and *Germinal* (F 735)
**Remarks:** named after the months of the French Revolutionary calendar, all six ships of the Floréal class were commissioned between 1992 and 1994, and were fully designed by the ship yard of Chantiers de l'Atlantique, Saint Nazaire, to specifications of the French navy as ocean-capable patrol vessels. They were built to passenger-ship standards with air conditioning and stabilisers, enabling them to operate a helicopter at up to sea state 5.

*Floréal*, the leader of the class, is stationed in the South Indian Ocean, and the other ships in various areas in the Far East where France has interests, including the sensitive nuclear test site of Mururoa Atoll

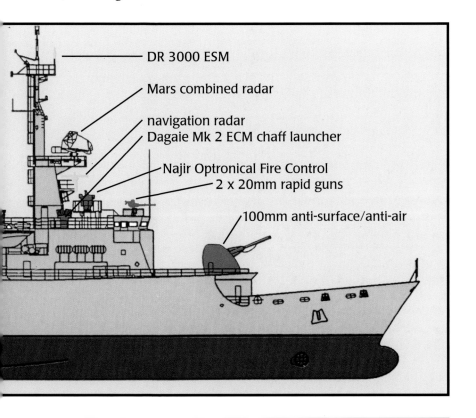

DR 3000 ESM

Mars combined radar

navigation radar
Dagaie Mk 2 ECM chaff launcher

Najir Optronical Fire Control
2 x 20mm rapid guns

100mm anti-surface/anti-air

# LA FAYETTE CLASS

**Type:** frigate (FFG)
**Country:** France
**Displacement:** 3,500 tons full load
**Dimensions:** length 125m (410.1ft); beam 15.4m (50.5ft); draught 4.4m (13.1ft)
**Gun armament:** one DNC 100mm (3.94in)/55 Mod 68 CADAM; two Giat 20F2 20mm (0.79in); two 12.7 (0.5in) MGs
**Missile armament:** eight Aerospatiale MM 40 Exocet SSM launchers; two octuple Thomson-CSF Crotale Naval CN 2 SAM launchers
**Electronics:** air/surface search; navigation; fire control radar systems
**Aircraft:** one Aerospatiale AS565 MA Panther helicopter
**Performance:** maximum speed 25kt
**Range:** 14,490km (9,000 miles) at 12kt
**Ships:** six; *La Fayette* (F 710), *Surcouf* (F 711), *Courbet* (F 712), *Jaureguiberry* (F 713), *Guepratte* (F 714), and *Ronarch* (F 715)

# BRANDENBURG (TYPE 123) CLASS

**Type:** frigate (FFG)
**Country:** Germany
**Displacement:** 4,700 tons full load
**Dimensions:** length 138.9m (455.7ft); beam 16.7m (54.8ft); draught 4.4m (14.4ft)
**Gun armament:** one OTO Melara 76mm (3in)/62
**Missile armament:** four Aerospatiale MM 38 Exocet SSM launchers; two RAM 21-cell Mk 49 SAM launchers
**Anti-submarine armament:** two twin 324mm (12.75in) tubes for Honeywell Mk 46 torpedoes
**Electronics:** air search; air/surface search; navigation; fire control radar systems, hull-mounted Atlas Elektronik DSQS 23BZ sonars
**Aircraft:** two Sea Lynx Mk 88 helicopters
**Propulsion:** two gas turbines and two diesels driving two shafts
**Performance:** maximum speed 29kt
**Range:** 6,440km (4,000 miles) at 18kt
**Complement:** 199 and 19 aircrew
**Ships:** four; *Brandenburg* (F 215), *Schleswig-Holstein* (F 216), *Bayern* (F 217), and *Mecklenburg-Vorpommern* (F 218)

**Above:** *the original SCHLESWIG-HOLSTEIN had been laid down in 1959 as a Hamburg class vessel designed as a general-purpose gun frigate optimised for anti-submarine warfare. The Brandenburgs were ordered in 1989, as a direct replacement for the Hamburgs, but with space on board allocated for a tank group commander and his battle staff*

# BREMEN (TYPE 122) CLASS

**Type:** frigate (FFG)
**Country:** Germany
**Displacement:** 3,600 tons full load
**Dimensions:** length 130.5m (428ft); beam 14.4m (47.2ft); draught 6m (19.7ft)
**Gun armament:** one OTO Melara 76mm(3in)/62 Mk 75
**Missile armament:** two quad launchers for McDonnell Douglas Harpoon SSMs; octuple launcher for Raytheon NATO Sea Sparrow SAMs
**Anti-submarine armament:** two twin 324mm (12.75in) tubes for Honeywell Mk 46 Mod 1 torpedoes

**Electronics:** air/surface search; navigation; fire control radar systems, hull-mounted Atlas Elektronik DSQS 21BZ sonars
**Aircraft:** two Westland Lynx MK 88 helicopters
**Propulsion:** two gas turbines and two diesels delivering power to two shafts
**Performance:** maximum speed 32kts on gas turbines or 20kt on diesels
**Range:** 7,400km (4,600 miles) at 18kt
**Complement:** 203
**Ships:** eight; *Bremen* (F 207), *Niedersachsen* (F 208), *Rheinland-Pfalz* (F 209), *Emden* (F 210), *Köln* (F 211), *Karlsruhr* (F 212), *Augsburg* (F 213), *Lübeck* (F 214)

***Below:*** *Bremen class frigates, which are modified Dutch Kortenaer designs, were ordered in 1977 with the first of class being commissioned in 1982*

# HYDRA (MEKO 200HN) CLASS

**Type:** frigate (FFG)
**Country:** Greece
**Displacement:** 3,200 tons full load
**Dimensions:** length 117m (383.9ft); beam 14.8m (48.6ft); draught 4.1m (13.5ft)
**Gun armament:** one FMC Mk 45 Mod 2A 127mm (5in)/54; two GD/GE Vulcan Phalanx 20mm (0.79in) Mk 15 Mod 12
**Missile armament:** two quad McDonnell Douglas Harpoon SSM launchers; Raytheon NATO Sea Sparrow Mk 48 SAM vertical launcher
**Torpedoes:** two triple 324mm (12.75in) Mk 32 Mod 5 tube mountings for Honeywell Mk 46 A/S torpedoes
**Aircraft:** one Sikorsky Aegean Hawk ASW helicopter
**Electronics:** air search; air/surface search; navigation; fire control radars, hull-mounted Raytheon SQS-56/DE 1160 sonar
**Propulsion:** two gas turbines, two diesels delivering to two shafts
**Performance:** maximum speed 31kt
**Range:** 6,600km (4,100 miles) at 16kt
**Complement:** 173
**Ships:** four; *Hydra* (F 452), *Spetsai* (F 453), *Psara* (F 454), and *Salamis* (F 455)

# GODAVARI CLASS

**Type:** frigate (FFG)
**Country:** India
**Displacement:** 3,850 tons full load
**Dimensions:** length 126.5m (414.9ft); beam 14.5m (47.6ft); draught 4.5m (14.8ft)
**Gun armament:** twin 56mm (2.2in)/70; four twin 30mm (1.18in)/65
**Missile armamant:** four SS-N-2D styx SSM launchers; twin SA-N-4 Gecko SAM launcher
**Torpedoes:** two triple 324mm (12.75in) ILAS tubes for Whitehead A244S
**Aircraft:** two Sea King or one Sea King and one Chetak helicopter
**Electronics:** air search; air/surface search; navigation; fire control radars, sonar
**Performance:** maximum speed 27kt
**Range:** 7,245km (4,500 miles) at 12kt
**Complement:** 330
**Ships:** three; *Godavari* (F 20), *Gomati* (F 21), and *Ganga* (F 22)

**Above:** *Meko 200 frigates were also used by the Turkish navy; known as Yavuz class, they were Meko 200T vessels. Class leader* YAVUZ *(F 240) is illustrated*

# FATAHILLAH CLASS

**Type:** frigate (FFH)
**Country:** Indonesia
**Displacement:** 1,450 tons full load
**Dimensions:** length 84m (276ft); beam 11.1m (36.4ft); draught 3.3m (10.7ft)
**Gun armament:** one Bofors 120mm (4.7in)/46; one or two Bofors 40mm (1.57in)/70; two Rheinmetall 20mm (0.79in)
**Missile armament:** four Aerospatiale MM 38 Exocet SSM launchers
**Torpedoes:** two triple 324mm (12.75in) tubes for Mk 44/46 A/S torpedoes
**Aircraft:** one Westland Wasp helicopter on *Nala* only
**Electronics:** Signaal DA 05 air/surface search; Racal Decca AC 1229 surface search; Signaal WM 28 fire control radars, and hull-mounted Signaal sonar
**Propulsion:** one gas turbine, two diesels delivering power to two shafts
**Performance:** maximum speed 30kt
**Range:** 6,842km (4,250 miles) at 16kt
**Complement:** 89
**Ships:** three; *Fatahillah* (361), *Malahayati* (362), and *Nala* (363)

# TRIBAL CLASS

**Type:** frigate (FFG)
**Country:** Indonesia
**Displacement:** 2,700 tons full load
**Dimensions:** length 109.7m (360ft); beam 13m (42.5ft); draught 3.8m (12.5ft)
**Gun armament:** two Vickers 114mm (4.5in)/55 Mk 8; two Oerlikon 20mm (0.79in); two 12.7mm (0.5in) MGs
**Missile armament:** two quad Short Bros Seacat SAM launchers
**Aircraft:** one Westland Wasp helicopter
**Electronics:** Marconi Type 965 air search; Type 993 surface search; Decca 978 navigation; Plessey Type 903 fire control radars, and hull-mounted Graseby Type 177 and Type 170B sonars
**Performance:** maximum speed 25kt
**Range:** 8,694km (5,400 miles) at 12kt
**Ships:** three; *Martha Kristina Tiyahahu* (331), ex HMS *Zulu*; *Wilhelmus Zakarias Yohannes* (332), ex HMS *Gurkha*, and *Hasanuddin* (333), ex HMS *Tartar*

# VAN SPEIJK CLASS

**Type:** frigate (FFG)
**Country:** Indonesia
**Displacement:** 2,835 tons full load
**Dimensions:** length 113.4m (372ft); beam 12.5m (41ft); draught 4.2m (13.8ft)
**Gun armament:** one OTO Melara 76mm (3in)/62 compact
**Missile armament:** eight McDonnell Douglas Harpoon SSM launchers; two quad Short Bros Sea Cat SAM launchers
**Torpedoes:** two triple 324mm (12.75in) Mk 32 tubes for Honeywell Mk 46
**Aircraft:** one Westland Wasp HAS.Mk 1 helicopter
**Electronics:** air-search; air/surface search; navigation; fire-control radar systems, and attack hull-mounted Signaal CWE 610 sonar
**Propulsion:** two sets of geared turbines delivering power to two shafts
**Performance:** maximum speed 28.5kt
**Range:** 7,245km (4,500 miles) at 12kt
**Ships:** six; *Ahmed Yani* (351), *Slamet Riyadi* (352), *Yos Sudarso* (353), *Oswald Siahaan* (354), *Abdul Halim Perdana Kusuma* (355), and *Karel Satsuitubun* (356)

# ALVAND CLASS

**Type:** frigate (FF)
**Country:** Iran
**Displacement:** 1,350 tons full load
**Dimensions:** length 94.5m (310ft); beam 11.1m (36.4ft); draught 4.3m (14.1ft)
**Gun armament:** one Vickers 114mm (4.5in)/55 Mk 8; twin Oerlikon 35mm (1.38in)/90; three Oerlikon GAM-B01 20mm (0.79in); two 12.7mm (0.5in) MGs
**Missile armament:** quintuple Sistal Sea Killer II launcher
**Electronics:** Plessey AWS 1 air/surface search; Racal Decca 1226 surface search; Decca 629 navigation; two Contraves Sea Hunter fire-control radar systems, Graseby 174 and 170 hull-mounted sonars
**Propulsion:** two gas turbines for high speed, two diesels for long-range cruising, delivering power to two shafts
**Performance:** maximum speed 39kt
**Range:** 5,876km (3,650 miles) at 18kt
**Complement:** 125
**Ships:** three; *Alvand* (71), ex *Saam*; *Alborz* (72), ex *Zaal*, and *Sabalan* (73),ex *Rostam*

# **LUPO** CLASS

**Type:** frigate (FFG)
**Country:** Italy
**Displacement:** 2,210 tons standard and 2,500 tons full load
**Dimensions:** length 113.2m (371.3ft); beam 11.3m (37.1ft); draught 3.7m (12.1ft)
**Gun armament:** one OTO Melara 127mm (5in)/54; two twin Breda 40mm (1.57in)/70 compact
**Missile armament:** eight OTO Melara Teseo Mk 2 (TG 2) SSM launchers; Raytheon NATO Sea Sparrow Mk 29 octuple SAM launcher
**Torpedoes:** two triple 324mm (12.75in) Mk 32 tubes for Honeywell Mk 46
**Aircraft:** one AB 212ASW helicopter
**Electronics:** air-search; surface search/target indication; surface search; navigation; fire-control radar systems, and hull-mounted Raytheon sonar
**Propulsion:** two diesels, two gas turbines delivering power to two shafts
**Performance:** maximum speed 35kt
**Range:** 7,000km (4,350 miles) at 16kt on diesels
**Complement:** 185
**Ships:** four; *Lupo* (F 564)  *Sagittario* (F 565)  *Perseo* (F 566), and *Orsa* (567), *illustrated below*

# MAESTRALE CLASS

**Type:** frigate (FFG)
**Country:** Italy
**Displacement:** 2,500 tons standard and 3,200 tons full load
**Dimensions:** length 122.7m (405ft); beam 12.9m (42.5ft); draught 8.4m (27.4ft) to screws
**Gun armament:** one OTO Melara 127mm (5in)/54 automatic; two twin Breda four 40mm (1.57in)/70 compact; two Oerlikon 20mm (0.79in)
**Missile armament:** four OTO Melara Teseo Mk 2 (TG 2) SSM launchers; Selenia Albatros octuple SAM launcher
**Torpedoes:** two triple 324mm (12.75in) Mk 32 tubes for Honeywell Mk 46
**Aircraft:** two AB 212ASW helicopters
**Electronics:** air/surface search; surface search; navigation; fire-control radar systems, and hull-mounted Raytheon DE 1164 sonar
**Propulsion:** two diesels, two gas turbines delivering power to two shafts
**Performance:** maximum speed 32kt
**Range:** 9,660km (6,000 miles) at 16kt
**Complement:** 224
**Ships:** eight; *Maestrale* (F 570), *Grecale* (F 571), *Libeccio* (F 572), *illustrated below*, *Scirocco* (F 573), *Aliseo* (F 575), *Euro* (F 575), *Espero* (F 576), and *Zeffiro* (F 577)

# ABUKUMA CLASS

**Type:** frigate (FF)
**Country:** Japan
**Displacement:** 2,550 tons full load
**Dimensions:** length 109m (357.6ft); beam 13.4m (44ft); draught 3.8m (12.5ft)
**Gun armament:** one OTO Melara 76mm (3in)/62 compact; one GE/GD 20mm (0.79in) Phalanx CIWS Mk 15
**Missile armament:** two quad McDonnell Douglas Harpoon SSM launchers
**Torpedoes:** two triple 324mm (12.75in) Type 68 tubes for Honeywell Mk 46 Mod 5 Neartip torpedoes
**Electronics:** Malco OPS 14C air search; JRC OPS 28 surface search; Type 2-21 fire-control radar systems, and hull-mounted Hitachi OQS-8 sonar
**Propulsion:** two gas turbines, two diesels delivering power to two shafts
**Performance:** maximum speed 27kt
**Range:** 6,485km (4,028 miles)
**Complement:** 120
**Ships:** six; *Abukuma* (DE 229), *Jintsu* (DE 230), *Ohyodo* (DE 231), *Sendai* (DE 232), *Chikuma* (DE 233), and *Tone* (DE 234)

# CHIKUGO CLASS

**Type:** frigate (FF)
**Country:** Japan
**Displacement:** 1,470–1,500 tons standard
**Dimensions:** length 93m (305ft); beam 10.8m (35.5ft); draught 3.5m (11.5ft)
**Gun armament:** twin USN 76mm (3in)/50; twin Bofors 40mm (1.57in)/60
**Torpedoes:** two triple 324mm (12.75in) tubes for Honeywell Neartip
**Electronics:** Melco OPS 14 air search; JRC OPS 16 surface search; Type 1B fire-control radar systems, and hull-mounted Hitachi OQS 3A sonar
**Propulsion:** diesels delivering power to twin screws
**Performance:** maximum speed 25kt
**Range:** 17,550km (10,900 miles) at 12kt
**Complement:** 165
**Ships:** eleven; *Chikugo* (DE 215), *Ayase* (DE 216), *Mikuma* (DE 217), *Tokachi* (DE 218), *Iwase* (DE 219), *Chitose* (DE 220), *Niyodo* (DE 221), *Teshio* (DE 222), *Yoshino* (DE 223), *Kumano* (DE 224), and *Noshiro* (DE 225)

# NAJIN CLASS

**Type:** frigate (FF)
**Country:** Korea, North
**Displacement:** 1,500 tons full load
**Dimensions:** length 102m (334.6ft); beam 10m (32.8ft); draught 2.7m (8.9ft)
**Gun armament:** two 100mm (3.94in)/56; two twin 57mm (2.24in)/80; two quad 25mm (1in)/70; four twin 14.5mm (0.57in) MGs
**Missile armament:** two SS-N-2A Styx SSM launchers
**Electronics:** Slim Net air search; Pot Head surface search; Pot Drum navigation; Drum Tilt fire-control radar systems, and hull-mounted and VDS type sonar
**Performance:** maximum speed 24kt
**Range:** 6,440km (4,000 miles) at 13kt
**Ships:** two; *Najin* (531) + one other

# ULSAN CLASS

**Type:** frigate (FF)
**Country:** Korea, South
**Displacement:** 2,180 tons full load
**Dimensions:** length 102m (334.6ft); beam 11.5m (37.7ft); draught 3.5m (11.5ft)
**Gun armament:** two OTO Melara 76mm (3in)/62 compact; four twin Emerson Electric 30mm (1.18in); six Breda 40mm (1.57in)/70
**Missile armament:** four twin McDonnell Douglas Harpoon SSM launchers
**Torpedoes:** two triple 324mm (12.75in) Mk 32 tubes for Honeywell Mk 46 Mod 1
**Electronics:** Signaal DA 05 air/surface search; Signaal ZW 06 or Marconi S 1810 surface search; Raytheon SPS 10C navigation; Signaal WM 28 or Marconi ST 1802 fire control radar systems, Signaal PHS 32 hull-mounted sonar
**Propulsion:** two diesels, two gas turbines delivering power to two shafts
**Performance:** maximum speed 34kt
**Range:** 6,440km (4,000 miles) at 15kt
**Complement:** 150
**Ships:** nine; *Ulsan* (FF 951), *Seoul* (FF 952), *Chung Nam* (FF 953), *Masan* (FF 955), *Kyong Buk* (FF 956), *Dhon Nam* (FF 957), *Che Ju* (FF 958), *Busan* (FF 959), and *Chung Ju* (FF 961)

# LEKIU CLASS

**Type:** frigate (FFG)
**Country:** Malaysia
**Displacement:** 2,270 tons full load
**Dimensions:** length 105.5m (346ft); beam 12.8m (42ft); draught 3.6m (11.8ft)
**Gun armament:** one Bofors 57mm (2.24in)/70 SAK Mk 2; two MSI Defense Systems 30mm (1.18in) DS 30B
**Missile armament:** eight Aerospatiale MM 40 Exocet SSM launchers; British Aerospace VLS Seawolf SAM launcher
**Torpedo armament:** two triple 324mm (12.75in) Whitehead B 515 tubes
**Aircraft:** one Westland Wasp HAS helicopter
**Electronics:** Signaal DA 08 air search; Erickson Sea Giraffe 150HC surface search; Racal I Band navigation; two Marconi 1802 fire control radar systems, Thomson Sintra Spherion hull-mounted sonar
**Performance:** maximum speed 28kt
**Range:** 8,050km (5,000 miles) at 14kt
**Ships:** two, *Lekiu* (30) and *Jebat* (29)

# RAHMAT CLASS

**Type:** frigate (FF)
**Country:** Malaysia
**Displacement:** 1,600 tons full load
**Dimensions:** length 93.9m (308ft); beam 10.4m (34.1ft); draught 4.5m (14.8ft)
**Gun armament:** one Vickers 114mm (4.5in)/45 Mk 5; three Bofors 40mm (1.57in)/70
**Anti-submarine armament:** one Limbo Mk 10 three-tubed mortar
**Electronics:** Signaal LW 02 air search; Decca 626 surface search; Kelvin Hughes MS 32 navigation; Signaal M 22 fire control radar systems, Graseby Type 170B and Type 174 hull-mounted sonars
**Performance:** maximum speed 26kt
**Range:** 9,660km (6,000 miles) at 16kt
**Ships:** one, *Rahmat* (24), ex *Hang Jebat*
**Remarks:** *Rahmat* has a unique maindeck overhang that falls short of the quarterdeck. The forward superstructure contains a pyramid mainmast on top, which supports the fire control radar dome

# JACOB VAN HEEMSKERCK CLASS

**Type:** frigate (FFG)
**Country:** Netherlands
**Displacement:** 3,750 tons full load
**Dimensions:** length 130.5m (428ft); beam 14.6m (47.9ft); draught 4.3m (14.1ft)
**Gun armament:** one Signaal SGE-30 Goalkeeper with General Electric 30mm (1.18in); two Orelikon 20mm (0.79in)
**Missile armament:** two quad McDonnell Douglas Harpoon SSM launchers; Mk 13 Mod 1 launcher for 40 GDC Pomona Standard SM-1MR SAMs; octuple launcher for Raytheon Sea Sparrow Mk 29 SAMs
**Torpedoes:** two twin US Mk 32 324mm (12.75in) tubes for Honeywell Mk 46 Mod 5 torpedoes
**Electronics:** air search; air/surface search; surface search; fire control radar systems, Westinghouse SQS 509 hull-mounted sonar
**Propulsion:** four gas turbines delivering power to two shafts
**Performance:** maximum speed 30kt
**Range:** 7,567km (4,700 miles) at 16kt
**Ships:** two; *Jacob Van Heemskerck* (F 812) and *Witte De With* (F 813)

*Below: WITTE DE WITH photographed in 1986, the year in which she was commissioned*

# KAREL DOORMAN CLASS

**Type:** frigate (FFG)
**Country:** Netherlands
**Displacement:** 3,320 tons full load
**Dimensions:** length 122.3m (401.1ft); beam 14.4m (47.2ft); draught 4.3m (14.1ft)
**Gun armament:** one OTO Melara 76mm (3in)/62 compact Mk 100; one Signaal SGE-30 Goalkeeper with General Electric 30mm (1.18in); two Oerlikon 20mm (0.79in)
**Missile armament:** two quad McDonnell Douglas Harpoon SSM launchers; vertical launchers for Raytheon Sea Sparrow Mk 48 SAMs
**Torpedoes:** two twin US Mk 32 324mm (12.75in) tubes for Honeywell Mk 46 Mod 5 torpedoes
**Aircraft:** one Westland SH-14 Lynx helicopter
**Electronics:** Signaal SMART and Signaal LW 08 air/surface search; Signaal ZW 06 surface search; Racal Decca 1226 navigation; two Signaal STIR fire control radar systems, Signaal PHS hull-mounted sonar and Thomson Sintra Anaconda DSBV 61 towed-array
**Performance:** maximum speed 30kt
**Range:** 8,050km (5,000 miles) at 18kt
**Complement:** 24 + 208
**Ships:** eight; *Karel Doorman* (F 827), *Willem Der Zaan* (F 829), *Tjerk Hiddes* (F 830), *Van Amstel* (F 831), *Abraham Van Der Hulst* (F 832), *Van Nes* (F 833), *Van Galen* (F 834), and *Van Speijk* (F 828)
**Remarks:** the Karel Doorman class vessels all have a distinctive pedestal-mounted air/surface search radar aerial at the forward end of the after structure, a large hangar with CIWS mounting on top at the after end, and a long flight deck, below which is an open quarterdeck

*Right:* KORTENAER *(F 807), which was laid down in April 1975 and commissioned in October 1978, is the leader of the seven-vessel Kortenaer class, which also comprises* PIET HEYN *(F 811),* ABRAHAM CRIJNSSEN *(F 816),* PHILIPS VAN ALMONDE *(F 823),* BLOYS VAN TRESLONG *(F 824),* JAN VAN BRAKEL *(F 825), and* PIETER FLORISZ *(F 826), ex* WILLEM VAN DER ZAAN. *The vessels are identical in hull and basic profile to the Jacob Van Heemskerck class. They are an excellent and versatile anti-submarine frigate design with additional useful anti-ship capability. The original intention was for a complement of 200, but the introduction of the Goalkeeper CIWS mounting and increased automation has reduced this figure to 167*

# KORTENAER CLASS

**Type:** frigate (FFG)
**Country:** Netherlands
**Displacement:** 3,050 tons standard and 3,630 tons full load
**Dimensions:** length 130.5m (428.1ft); beam 14.6m (47.9ft); draught 4.3m (14.1ft)
**Gun armament:** one OTO Melara 76mm (3in)/62 compact; one Signaal SGE-30 Goalkeeper with General Electric 30mm (1.18in); two Oerlikon 20mm (0.79in)
**Missile armament:** two quad McDonnell Douglas Harpoon SSM launchers; octuple Raytheon Sea Sparrow Mk 29 SAM launcher
**Torpedoes:** two twin US Mk 32 324mm (12.75in) tubes for Honeywell Mk 46 Mod 5 torpedoes
**Aircraft:** two Westland SH-14B Lynx helicopters
**Electronics:** Signaal LW 08 air search; Signaal ZW 06 surface search; Signaal STIR and WM 25 fire control radar systems, Westinghouse bow-mounted sonar
**Propulsion:** two gas turbines delivering power to two shafts
**Performance:** maximum speed 30kt
**Range:** 7,567km (4,700 miles) at 16kt
**Complement:** 167
**Ships:** seven

# **TROMP** CLASS

**Type:** frigate (FFG)
**Country:** Netherlands
**Displacement:** 4,308 tons full load
**Dimensions:** length 138.2m (453.3ft); beam 14.8m (48.6ft); draught 4.6m (15.1ft)
**Gun armament:** twin Bofors 120mm (4.7in/50; Signaal SGE-30mm (1.18in Goalkeeper; two Oerlikon 20mm (0.79in)
**Missile armament:** two quad McDonnell Douglas Harpoon SSM launchers; octuple Raytheon Sea Sparrow Mk 29 SAM launcher; GDC Pomona Standard SAM launcher
**Torpedoes:** two triple US Mk 32 324mm (12.75in) tubes for Honeywell Mk 46 Mod 5 torpedoes
**Aircraft:** one Westland SH-14B Lynx helicopter
**Electronics:** air/surface search; navigation; fire control radar systems, hull-mounted CWE 6 10 sonar
**Performance:** maximum speed 30kt
**Range:** 8,050km (5,000 miles) at 18kt
**Ships:** two; *Tromp* (F 801) and *De Ruyter* (F 806)

# LEANDER CLASS

**Type:** frigate (FFH)
**Country:** New Zealand
**Displacement:** 3,035 tons full load (Broad-beamed type 2,945 tons)
**Dimensions:** length 113.4m (372ft); beam 12.5m (41ft) [Broad-beamed 13.1m (43ft)]; draught 5.5m (18ft)
**Gun armament:** twin Vickers 114mm (4.5in)/45 [two Bofors 40mm (1.57in)/60 in *Southland*]; four or six 12.7mm (0.5in) MGs
**Torpedoes:** two triple US Mk 32 Mod 5 tubes for Honeywell/Marconi Mk 46 Mod 2 torpedoes
**Aircraft:** one Westland Wasp HAS 1 helicopter
**Electronics:** air search; air/surface search; navigation; fire-control radar systems, hull-mounted sonar
**Performance:** maximum speed 28kt
**Range:** 4,830km (3,000 miles) at 15kt [Broad-beam 8,855km (5,500miles) at 15kt]
**Ships:** four; *Waikato* (F 55); *Wellington** (F 69), ex HMS *Bacchante*; *Southland* (F 104), ex HMS *Dido, illustrated below*, and *Canterbury** (F 421)
* indicates vessels are Broad-beam type

# **OSLO** CLASS

**Type:** frigate (FFG)
**Country:** Norway
**Displacement:** 1,450 tons standard and 1,745 tons full load
**Dimensions:** length 96.6m (317ft); beam 11.2m (36.7ft); draught 5.5m (18ft)
**Gun armament:** two US 76mm (3in)/50; one Bofors 40mm (1.57in)/70; two Rheinmetall 20mm (0.79in)/20
**Missile armament:** four Penguin Mk 2 SSM launchers; octuple Raytheon Sea Sparrow SAM launcher
**Torpedoes:** two triple 324mm (12.75in) US Mk 32 tubes for Marconi Stingray
**Electronics:** air-search; surface-search; navigation; fire-control radar systems, combined hull-mounted and VDS sonars
**Propulsion:** two boilers supplying steam to one set of geared turbines delivering 14,915kW (20,000shp) to one shaft
**Performance:** maximum speed 25+kt
**Range:** 7,245km (4,500 miles) at 15kt
**Complement:** 11 + 139
**Ships:** four; *Bergen* (F 301), *Trondheim* (F 302), *Stavanger* (F 303), and *Narvik* (F 304)

# **KASZUB** CLASS

**Type:** frigate (FF)
**Country:** Poland
**Displacement:** 1,183 tons full load
**Dimensions:** length 82.3m (270ft); beam 10m (32.8ft); draught 3.1m (10.2ft)
**Gun armament:** one USSR 76mm (3in/66; three twin Wrobel 23mm (0.9in)/87
**Missile armament:** two quad SA-N-5 SAM launchers
**Torpedoes:** two twin 533mm (21in) tubes
**Electronics:** Strut Curve air/surface search; Tamirio RN 231 surface search, dipping type sonar mounted on a transom at the stern
**Performance:** maximum speed 26kt
**Range:** 3,220km (2,000 miles) at 18kt
**Ships:** one, *Kaszub* (240)

*Below:* the Oslo class frigate, STAVANGER, was commissioned in December 1967, having been laid down in 1965 two years after the lead of class OSLO. The latter unfortunately sank in 1994 after running aground following a complete engine failure. All of the ships in the class were built by Marienes Hovedverft

# BAPTISTA DE ANDRADE CLASS

**Type:** frigate (FF)
**Country:** Portugal
**Displacement:** 1,380 tons full load
**Dimensions:** length 84.6m (277.5ft); beam 10.3m (33.8ft); draught 3.1m (10.2ft)
**Gun armament:** one Creusot Loire 100mm (3.94in)/55; two Bofors 40mm (1.57in)/70
**Torpedoes:** two triple 324mm (12.75in) US Mk 32 tubes for Honeywell Mk 46
**Aircraft:** provision for one Westland Lynx helicopter
**Electronics:** air/surface search; navigation; fire-control radar systems, hull-mounted Thomson Sintra Diodon sonar
**Propulsion:** two diesels driving two shafts
**Performance:** maximum speed 22kt
**Complement:** 122
**Range:** 9,500km (5,900 miles) at 18kt
**Ships:** four; *Baptista De Andrade* (F 486), *João Roby* (F 487), *Afonson Cerqueira* (F 488), and *Oliveira Carmo* (F 489)

# COMANDANTE JOÃO BELO CLASS

**Type:** frigate (FF)
**Country:** Portugal
**Displacement:** 1,750 tons standard and 2,250 tons full load
**Dimensions:** length 102.7m (336.9ft); beam 11.7m (38.4ft); draught 4.4m (14.4ft)
**Gun armament:** three Creusot Loire 100mm (3.94in)/55; two Bofors 40mm (1.57in)/60
**Torpedoes:** two triple 550mm (21.65in) tubes
**Electronics:** air search; surface search; navigation; fire-control radar systems, hull-mounted sonars
**Propulsion:** four diesels driving two shafts
**Performance:** maximum speed 25kt
**Complement:** 14 + 186
**Range:** 12,075km (7,500 miles) at 15kt
**Ships:** four; *Comandante João Belo* (F 480), *Comandante Hermenegildo Capelo* (F 481), *Comandante Roberto Ivens* (F 482), and *Comandante Sacadura Cabral* (F 483)

# *VASCO DA GAMA* CLASS

**Type:** frigate (FFG)
**Country:** Portugal
**Displacement:** 3,300 tons full load
**Dimensions:** length 115.9m (380.3ft); beam 14.8m (48.7ft); draught 6.1m (20ft)
**Gun armament:** one Creusot Loire 100mm (3.94in)/55; one GE/GD Vulcan Phalanx 20mm (0.79in) Mk 15 Mod 11
**Missile armament:** two quad McDonnell Douglas Harpoon SSM launchers; octuple Raytheon Sea Sparrow Mk 29 launcher
**Torpedoes:** two triple 324mm (12.75in) US Mk 32 tubes for Honeywell Mk 46
**Electronics:** air search; air/surface search; navigation; fire control radar systems, hull-mounted Computing Devices (Canada) SQS 5 10(V) sonar
**Performance:** maximum speed 32kt
**Range:** 15,456km (9,600 miles) at 12kt
**Ships:** three; *Vasco da Gama* (F 330), *Alvares Cabral* (F 331), and *Corte Real* (F 332)

*Below:* COMANDANTE JOÃO BELO *was laid down in 1965 and commissioned in 1967. The other ships in the class were all commissioned within a further two years*

# TETAL CLASS

**Type:** frigate (FF)
**Country:** Romania
**Displacement:** 1,440 tons full load
**Dimensions:** length 95.4m (303.1ft); beam 11.7m (38.4ft); draught 3m (9.8ft)
**Gun armament:** two or four USSR 76mm (3in)/60; two twin USSR 30mm (1.18in)/65; two 14.5mm (0.57in) MGs
**Torpedoes:** two twin 533mm (21in) tubes for Soviet Type 53 torpedoes
**Electronics:** Strut Curve air/surface search; Drum Tilt and Hawk Screech fire-control radar systems, hull-mounted sonar
**Performance:** maximum speed 24kt
**Ships:** six; *Admiral Petre Barbuneanu* (260), *Vice Admiral Vasile Scodrea* (261), *Vice Admiral Vasile Urseanu* (262), *Vice Admiral Eugeniu Rosca* (263), *Contre Admiral Eustatiu Sebastian* (264) + one other

# GEPARD CLASS

**Type:** frigate (FFG)
**Country:** Russia and associated states
**Displacement:** 1,900 tons full load
**Dimensions:** length 102m (334.6ft); beam 13.6m (44.6ft); draught 4.4m (14.4ft)
**Gun armament:** one 76mm (3in)/60; two ADG630 30mm (1.18in)/65
**Missile armament:** two quad Zvezda SS-N-25 SSM launchers; twin SA-N-4 Gecko SAM launcher
**Torpedoes:** two twin 533mm (21in) tubes for Soviet Type 53 torpedoes
**Electronics:** Cross Dome and Band Stand air/surface search; Nayada navigation; Bass Tilt and Pop Group fire-control radar systems, hull-mounted sonar
**Propulsion:** two gas turbines and two diesels driving two shafts
**Performance:** maximum speed 26kt
**Range;** 5,635km (3,500 miles) at 18kt
**Complement:** 110
**Ships:** one, *Zelenodolsk*
**Remarks:** the only ship in the class was laid down in 1991 and commissioned in July 1993; there was to have been a second ship, but this was scrapped owing to lack of funds

# GRISHA I-V CLASS

**Type:** frigate (FFG)
**Country:** Russia and associated states
**Displacement:** 1,200 tons full load
**Dimensions:** length 72m (236.2ft); beam 10m (32.8ft); draught 3.7m (12.1ft)
**Gun armament:** twin 57mm (2.24in)/80 (two twin in Grisha II class); one 76mm (3in)/60 (in Grisha V class only); one 30mm (1.18in)/65 (Grisha III and V classes only)
**Missile armament:** twin SA-N-4 Gecko SAM launcher ( Grisha I, III, V classes)
**Torpedoes:** two twin 533mm (21in) tubes for Type 53 torpedoes
**Electronics:** Strut Curve air/surface search (Strut Pair or Half Plate Bravo in Grisha V class); Don 2 navigation radar; Pop Group (except in Grisha II class), Muff Cob (in Grisha I, II classes), Bass Tilt (in Grisha III and IV classes) fire-control radar systems, hull-mounted sonars
**Propulsion:** one gas turbine and four diesels delivering power to three shafts
**Performance:** maximum speed 30kt
**Range:** 4,025km (2,500 miles) at 14kt
**Complement:** 80
**Ships:** fourteen Grisha I; eight Grisha II; twenty-eight Grisha III, and thirty Grisha V
**Remarks:** the original anti-submarine Grisha I class vessels were built between 1968 and 1974, and were followed by the border patrol Grisha II ships which were assigned to the Maritime Border Directorate of the KGB. The Grisha III class ships were the main production model for the Soviet Navy and they were constructed in the early 1980s.

Russia sold two Grisha II vessels to Lithuania in 1992, transferred a further four to the Ukraine in 1994, and delivered a Grisha V class vessel to the Ukraine in 1996.

The main recognition features of the original Grisha I class ships are:
• High bow with sweeping lines to the stern;
• Pyramid-type mainmast at the after end of the forward superstructure;
• Small Y-shaped lattice mast at the top of, and behind, the mainmast;
• Pop Group fire control radar system aerial on top of the forward
   superstructure and forward of the mainmast;
• Single, low profile, square-shaped funnel just aft of the midships;
• Muff Cob fire control radar aerial on top of the small after superstructure.
   The Grisha III ships are very similar except for the raised after superstructure which has the Bass Tilt fire control radar aerial on top.

# KRIVAK I-III CLASS

**Type:** frigate (FFG)
**Country:** Russia and associated states
**Displacement:** 3,600 tons full load (3,900 tons Krivak II and Krivak III class)
**Dimensions:** length 123.5m (405.2ft); beam 14m (45.9ft); draught 5m (16.4ft)
**Gun armament:** two twin 76mm (3in)/60 (in Krivak I only); two 100mm (3.94in)/59 (in Krivak II only, with one in Krivak III); two 30mm (1.18in)/65 (in Krivak III only)
**Missile armament:** two quad SS-N-25 SSM launchers (in Krivak I after modernisation); twin SA-N-4 Gecko SAM launchers (only one in Krivak III)
**Torpedoes:** two quad 533mm (21in) tubes for Type 53 torpedoes
**Aircraft:** one Kamov Ka-27 Helix A helicopter (Krivak III class only)
**Electronics:** air search; surface search; fire control radar systems, hull-mounted sonars
**Propulsion:** four gas turbines delivering power to two shafts
**Performance:** maximum speed 32kt
**Range:** 7,400km (4,600 miles) at 20kt
**Complement:** 220
**Ships:** nineteen Krivak I class, eleven Krivak II class, and nine Krivak III class

*Below: ZADORNY (959), a Krivak I class guided-missile escort frigate*

# NEUSTRASHIMY CLASS

**Type:** frigate (FFG)
**Country:** Russia and associated states
**Displacement:** 4,250 tons full load
**Dimensions:** length 129m (423.2ft); beam 15.5m (50.9ft); draught 4.8m (15.7ft)
**Gun armament:** one 100mm (3.94in)/70
**Missile armament:** two quad SS-N-25 SSM launchers; four vertical sextuple SA-N-9 Gauntlet SAM launchers; twin 30mm (1.18in) Gatling combined with eight SA-N-11 SAM/guns
**Torpedoes:** six 533mm (21in) tubes combined with A/S launcher for either SS-N-15 missiles or anti-submarine torpedoes
**Aircraft:** one Kamov Ka-27 Helix A helicopter on a deck that extends across the full width of the ship
**Electronics:** Top Plate, 3D air/surface search; two Palm Frond navigation; Cross Dome and Kite Search fire control radar systems, Bull Nose and hull-mounted Steer Hide VDS or towed-array sonar
**Propulsion:** four gas turbines driving two shafts
**Performance:** maximum speed 32kt
**Range:** 7,245km (4,500 miles) at 16kt
**Complement:** 210
**Ships:** two; *Neustrashimy*, and *Yaroslavl Mudry*

# PARCHIM CLASS

**Type:** frigate (FFG)
**Country:** Russia and associated states
**Displacement:** 1,200 tons full load
**Dimensions:** length 75.2m (246.7ft); beam 9.8m (32.2ft); draught 4.4m (14.4ft)
**Gun armament:** one 76mm (3in)/66; one six-barrelled 30mm (1.18in)/65
**Missile armament:** two quad SA-N-5 Grail SAM launchers
**Torpedoes:** four 533mm (21in) tubes for Type 53 torpedoes
**Electronics:** Cross Dome air/surface search; TSR 333 navigation; Bass Tilt fire control radar systems, hull-mounted sonar with helicopter-type VDS
**Performance:** maximum speed 28kt
**Ships:** twelve, with the following pennant numbers: MPK 67, MPK 99, MPK 105, MPK 192, MPK 205, MPK 213, MPK 216, MPK 219, MPK 224, MPK 228, and MPK 229; + one other

# MADINA CLASS

**Type:** frigate (FFG)
**Country:** Saudi Arabia
**Displacement:** 2,870 tons full load
**Dimensions:** length 115m (377.3ft); beam 12.5m (41ft); draught 4.9m (16ft)
**Gun armament:** one Creusot Loire 76mm (3in)/55; two twin Breda 40mm (1.57in)/70
**Missile armament:** two quad OTO Melara Otomat Mk 2 SSM launchers; octuple Thomson-CSF Crotale Naval SAM launcher
**Torpedoes:** four 533mm (21in) tubes for ECAN F17P torpedoes
**Aircraft:** one SA 365F Dauphin 2 helicopter
**Electronics:** air/surface search/IFF; navigation; fire control radar systems, hull-mounted sonar
**Propulsion:** four diesel engines delivering power to two shafts
**Performance:** maximum speed 30kt
**Range:** 12,880km (8,000 miles) at 15kt or 10,465km (6,500 miles) at 18kt
**Complement:** 179
**Ships:** four; *Madina* (702), *Hofouf* (704), *Abha* (706), and *Taif* (708)

*Below: the French-built* MADINA *was originally delivered in 1985, but has recently been upgraded and returned to service along with her sister ships*

# BALEARES CLASS

**Type:** frigate (FFG)
**Country:** Spain
**Displacement:** 4,177 tons full load
**Dimensions:** length 133.6m (438ft); beam 14.3m (46.9ft); draught 4.7m (15.4ft)
**Gun armament:** one FMC 127mm (5in)/54 Mk 42 Mod 9; two Brazán 20mm (0.79in)/120 twelve-barrelled Meroka
**Missile armament:** eight McDonnell Douglas Harpoon SSM launchers; sixteen GDC Pomona Standard SAM launchers
**Torpedoes:** four 324mm (12.75in) US Mk 32 tubes for Honeywell Mk 46 Mod 5 torpedoes; two 484mm (19in) US Mk 25 stern tubes for Westinghouse Mk 37
**Electronics:** air search; surface search; navigation; fire control radar systems, hull-mounted sonar
**Performance:** maximum speed 28kt
**Range:** 7,245km (4,500 miles) at 20kt
**Ships:** five; *Baleares* (F 71), *Andalucía* (F 72), *Cataluña* (F 73), *Asturias* (F 74), and *Extremadura* (F 75)

# DESCUBIERTA CLASS

**Type:** frigate (FFG)
**Country:** Spain
**Displacement:** 1,666 tons full load
**Dimensions:** length 88.8m (291.3ft); beam 10.4m (34ft); draught 3.8m (12.5ft)
**Gun armament:** one OTO Melara 76mm (3in)/62; one Bofors 40mm (1.57in)
**Missile armament:** two quad McDonnell Douglas Harpoon SSM launchers; octuple Selenia Albatros SAM launcher
**Torpedoes:** two triple 324mm (12.75in) US Mk 32 tubes for Honeywell Mk 46 Mod 5 torpedoes
**Electronics:** air/surface search; navigation; fire-control radar systems, Raytheon 1160B hull-mounted sonar
**Propulsion:** four diesels delivering 13,400kW (17,970shp) to two shafts
**Performance:** maximum speed 25kt
**Range:** 12,075km (7,500 miles) at 12kt
**Ships:** six; *Descubierta* (F 31), *Diana* (F 32), *Infanta Elena* (F 33), *Infanta Cristina* (F 34), *Cazadora* (F 35), and *Vencedora* (F 36)

# CHAO PHRAYA CLASS

**Type:** frigate (FF)
**Country:** Thailand
**Displacement:** 1,924 tons full load
**Dimensions:** length 103.2m (338.5ft); beam 11.3m (37.1ft); draught 3.1m (10.2ft)
**Gun armament:** two or four China 100mm (3.94in)/56; four twin China 37mm (1.46in)/76
**Missile armament:** eight Ying Ji (Eagle Strike) SSM launchers sited forward and aft of the funnel
**Electronics:** air/surface search; surface search/fire control; navigation; fire control radar systems, hull-mounted sonar
**Propulsion:** four diesel engines delivering power to two shafts
**Performance:** maximum speed 30kt
**Range:** 5,635km (3,500 miles) at 18kt
**Complement:** 168
**Ships:** four; *Chao Phraya* (455), *Bangpakong* (456), *Kraburi* (457), and *Saiburi* (458)

# NARESUAN CLASS

**Type:** frigate (FFG)
**Country:** Thailand
**Displacement:** 2,980 tons full load
**Dimensions:** length 120m (393.7ft); beam 13m (42.7ft); draught 3.8m (12.5ft)
**Gun armament:** one FMC 127mm (5in)/54 Mk 45 Mod 2; two twin China 37mm (1.46in)/62 H/PJ 76 A
**Missile armament:** two quad McDonnell Douglas Harpoon SSM launchers sited aft of forward superstructure; Mk 41 LCHR 8-cell SAM launcher
**Torpedoes:** two triple 324mm (12.75in) Mk 32 Mod 5 tubes for Honeywell Mk 46 torpedoes
**Aircraft:** one Kaman SH-2F Seasprite helicopter
**Electronics:** Signaal LW 08 air search; China Type 360 surface search; two Raytheon SPS 64(V)5 navigation; two Signaal STIR and China 374 G fire-control radar systems, China SJD-7 hull-mounted sonar
**Performance:** maximum speed 32kt
**Range:** 6,440km (4,000 miles) at 18kt
**Ships:** two; *Naresuan* (621) and *Taksin* (622)

# BARBAROS CLASS

**Type:** frigate (FFG)
**Country:** Turkey
**Displacement:** 3,350 tons full load
**Dimensions:** length 116.7m (382.9ft); beam 14.8m (48.6ft); draught 4.3m (14.1ft)
**Gun armament:** one FMC 127mm (5in)/54 Mk 45 Mod 2; three Oerlikon-Contraves 25mm (1in) Sea Zenith
**Missile armament:** eight McDonnell Douglas Harpoon SSM launchers; Raytheon Sea Sparrow Mk 29 Mod 1 SAM launchers
**Torpedoes:** two triple 324mm (12.75in) Mk 32 Mod 5 tubes for Honeywell Mk 46 torpedoes
**Aircraft:** one AB 212 ASW helicopter
**Electronics:** air search; air/surface search; navigation; fire control radar systems, Raytheon SQS 56 hull-mounted sonar
**Performance:** maximum speed 32kt
**Ships:** four; *Barbaros* (F 244), *Orucreis* (F 245), *Salihreis* (F 246), and *Kemalreis* (F 247)

# BROADSWORD CLASS (BATCH 1 AND 2)

**Type:** frigate (FFG)
**Country:** United Kingdom
**Displacement:** 4,400 tons full load
**Dimensions:** length 131.2m (430ft); beam 14.8m (48.5ft); draught 6m (19.9ft)
**Gun armament:** two twin Oerlikon/BMARC 30mm (1.18in)/75; two Oerlikon/BMARC 20mm (0.79in)
**Missile armament:** four Aerospatiale MM 38 Exocet SSM launchers; two British Aerospace six-barrelled Seawolf GWS 25 SAM launchers
**Torpedoes:** two triple 324mm (12.75in) Plessey STWS Mk 2 tubes for Marconi Stingray torpedoes
**Aircraft:** two Westland Lynx HAS 3 helicopters
**Electronics:** air/surface search; navigation; fire control radar systems, hull-mounted sonar
**Propulsion:** two gas turbines delivering power to two shafts
**Performance:** maximum speed 30kt
**Range:** 7,245km (4,500 miles) at 18kt
**Complement:** 286

**Above:** *the Broadsword class Batch 3 frigate,* CAMPBELTOWN, *which was built by Cammell Laird, was laid down in December 1985, launched in 1987 and commissioned in May 1989*

**Remarks:** four Type 22, or Broadsword class, Batch 1 ships were built. They were conceived as ASW ships for use from the Barents Sea to the North Atlantic, against high-performance Soviet nuclear submarines. All four were subsequently sold to Brazil; *Broadsword* (F 88) in 1995, *Brilliant* (F 90) and *Brazen* (F 91) in 1996, and *Battleaxe* (F 89) in 1997. Two of the six Batch 2 vessels, *London* and *Coventry*, were decommissioned in 2000 and are being sold to Romania

**Above:** six Batch 2 ships were commissioned in the 1980s, and were deployed with the 1st Frigate Squadron; they are BOXER (F 92), illustrated; BEAVER (F 93); BRAVE (F 94); LONDON (F 95), ex BLOODHOUND; SHEFFIELD (F 96), and COVENTRY (F 98)

# BROADSWORD CLASS (BATCH 3)

**Type:** frigate (FFG)
**Country:** United Kingdom
**Displacement:** 4,800 tons full load
**Dimensions:** length 148.1m (485.9ft); beam 14.8m (48.5ft); draught 6.4m (21ft)
**Gun armament:** one Vickers 114mm (4.5in)/55; two DES/Oerlikon 30mm (1.18in)/75; one 30mm (1.18in) seven-barrelled Goalkeeper CIWS mounting
**Missile armament:** two quad McDonnell Douglas Harpoon SSM launchers; two British Aerospace Sea Wolf GWS 25 Mod 3 SAM launchers
**Torpedoes:** two triple 324mm (12.75in) Plessey STWS Mk 2 tubes for Marconi Stingray torpedoes
**Aircraft:** usually two Westland Lynx HAS 3 but provision for EH101 Merlin
**Electronics:** Marconi Type 967/968 air/surface search; Kelvin Hughes Type 1006 or 1007 navigation; two Marconi Type 911 fire control radar systems, Plessey Type 2016 hull-mounted sonar and Dowty Type 2016 towed-array
**Propulsion:** four gas turbines delivering power to two shafts
**Performance:** maximum speed 30kt on Spey, and 18kt on Tyne engines
**Range:** 8,370km (5,200 miles) at 18kt on Tyne engines
**Complement:** 273
**Ships:** four; *Cornwall* (F 99), *Cumberland* (F 85), *Campbeltown* (F 86), *Chatham* (F 87)

# DUKE CLASS

**Type:** frigate (FFG)
**Country:** United Kingdom
**Displacement:** 3,500 tons standard and 4,200 tons full load
**Dimensions:** length 133m (436.2ft); beam 16.1m (52.8ft); draught 5.5m (18ft)
**Gun armament:** one Vickers 114mm (4.5in)/55; two Oerlikon 30mm (1.18in)/75
**Missile armament:** two quad McDonnell Douglas Harpoon SSM launchers; one British Aerospace Sea Wolf GWS 26 Mod 1 VLS SAM launcher
**Torpedoes:** two twin 324mm (12.75in) Cray Marine tubes for Marconi Stingray
**Aircraft:** one Westland Lynx HAS 3 or EH101 Merlin helicopter
**Electronics:** Plessey Type 996(I) 3D air/surface search; Kelvin Hughes Type 1007 navigation; two Marconi Type 911 fire control radar systems, Ferranti/Thomson Sintra Type 2050 bow-mounted sonar
**Propulsion:** two gas turbines and four diesels delivering power to two shafts
**Performance:** maximum speed 28kt
**Range:** 12,558km (7,800 miles) at 15kt
**Complement:** 17 + 168
**Ships:** thirteen; *Norfolk* (F 230), *illustrated below*; *Argyll* (F 231); *Lancaster* (F 229, ex F 232); *Marlborough* (F 233); *Iron Duke* (F 234); *Monmouth* (F 235); *Montrose* (F 236); *Westminster* (F 237); *Northumberland* (F 238); *Richmond* (F 239); *Somerset* (F 240); *Grafton* (F 241), and *Sutherland* (F 242)

# OLIVER HAZARD PERRY CLASS

**Type:** frigate (FFG)
**Country:** United States of America
**Displacement:** 4,100 tons full load
**Dimensions:** length 135.6m (445ft); beam 13.7m (45ft);
draught 4.5m (14.8ft) and 5.7m (24.5ft) to sonar dome
**Gun armament:** one OTO Melara 76mm (3in)/62 compact
in a Mk 75 single mounting; one GE/GD Vulcan Phalanx
20mm (0.79in) six-barrelled Mk 15 close-in weapon system
mounting; four 12.7mm (0.5in) MGs

**Missile armament:** four McDonnell
Douglas Harpoon SSM launchers;
GDC Standard SM-1MR SAM launcher
**Torpedoes:** two triple 324mm (12.75in) Mk 32 tubes
for Honeywell Mk 46 torpedoes
**Aircraft:** two Kaman SH-2F Seasprite helicopters
**Electronics:** air search; surface search/navigation;
fire control radar systems, hull-mounted sonar
**Propulsion:** two gas turbines delivering power to one shaft
**Performance:** maximum speed 29kt
**Range:** 8,370km (5,200 miles) at 20kt
**Complement:** 11 + 153 and an air unit strength of 46
**Ships:** fifty-one; *Oliver Hazard Perry* (FFG 7, ex PF 109) + 50

**Remarks:** this general-purpose class of frigates is one of the most significant frigate classes in the world. It was designed to escort merchant convoys or amphibious squadrons, and to provide area defence of surface vessels against attacking aircraft and cruise missiles, with anti-surface warfare as a secondary role. The first of class, *Oliver Hazard Perry*, was built by Bath Iron Works. It was laid down in 1975 and commissioned in 1977. All ships were built either by Bath Iron Works or Todd Pacific.

All ships feature a T Mk 6 Fanfare torpedo-decoy system, a Raytheon SLQ electronic countermeasures system, two OE-82 satellite communications antennae, a SRR-1 satellite communications receiver, and one WSC-3 satellite communications transceiver.

The ships supplied to Australia as the Adelaide class guided-missile frigates are, in all essential respects, similar to the US class.

*Left:* USS KAUFFMAN (FFG 59), which is one of the 51 United States Oliver Hazard Perry class general-purpose frigates. First launched in 1976, they were designed to escort merchant convoys

# CORVETTES

This term is generally used to describe ships below the frigate category. In the early seventeenth century, corvettes were of the order of 12.19–18.29m (40–60ft) in length and 40–70 tons displacement, and were armed with four to eight cannon, firing 1.4–1.8kg (3–4lb) balls. By the early 1700s their size had increased by another 6.1m (20ft) and 30 tons, and 100 years later they were often an impressive 400–600 tons, armed with 14.5kg (32lb) cannon.

During this time their numbers have varied widely; only the Royal Navy built to any great extent, though at the beginning of the twenty-first century it has no corvettes within the fleet. The type is popular with the navies of smaller nations for coastal patrol purposes, armed with Harpoon missiles and a helicopter. Many of these craft were built elsewhere, particularly by Russia, which itself still deploys around 100 corvettes. Included in this figure are the vessels of the 850-ton Nanuchka I class, which first appeared in 1969.

The Nanuchka ships were classed by the Russians as small rocket ships; to western observers they apeared to be coastal missile corvettes, although they were often seen quite far from home waters, a characteristic more of the light frigate category, especially considering their very impressive armament. Russia exported the later class of Nanuchkas to its then-regular customers, including India, Libya and Algeria.

# AL MANAMA CLASS

**Type:** corvette (FS)
**Country:** Bahrain
**Displacement:** 632 tons full load
**Dimensions:** length 63m (206.7ft); beam 9.3m (30.5ft); draught 2.9m (9.5ft)
**Gun armament:** one 76mm (3in); twin 40mm (1.57in); two 20mm (0.79in)
**Missile armament:** two twin Aerospatiale Exocet SSM launchers
**Performance:** maximum speed 32kt
**Range:** 6,440km (4,000 miles) at 16kt
**Ships:** two

# KRALJ CLASS

**Type:** corvette (FS)
**Country:** Croatia
**Displacement:** 385 tons full load
**Dimensions:** length 53.6m (175.9ft); beam 8.5m (27.9ft); draught 2.3m (7.5ft)
**Gun armament:** one 57mm (2.24in); one 30mm (1.18in); two 20mm (0.79in) MGs
**Missile armament:** four Saab RBS 15 SSM launchers
**Performance:** maximum speed 36kt
**Range:** 2,425km (1,500 miles) at 20kt
**Ships:** two

# ESMERALDAS CLASS

**Type:** corvette (FSG)
**Country:** Ecuador
**Displacement:** 685 tons full load
**Dimensions:** length 62.3m (204.4ft); beam 9.3m (30.5ft); draught 2.5m (8.2ft)
**Gun armament:** one OTO Melara 76mm (3in); two Breda 40mm (1.57in)
**Missile armament:** two triple Exocet SSM launchers; quad Aspide SAM launcher
**Torpedoes:** two triple 324mm (12.75in) tubes
**Aircraft:** one Bell 206B can be embarked
**Performance:** maximum speed 37kt
**Range:** 7,084km (4,400 miles) at 14kt
**Ships:** six, one of which, *Los Rios* (CM 13), is *illustrated left*

# TURUNMAA CLASS

**Type:** corvette (FS)
**Country:** Finland
**Displacement:** 770 tons full load
**Dimensions:** length 74.1m (243.1ft); beam 7.8m (25.6ft); draught 2.4m (7.9ft)
**Gun armament:** one 120mm (4.7in); twin 40mm (1.57in); twin 23mm (0.9in)
**Performance:** maximum speed 35kt
**Range:** 4,025km (2,500 miles) at 14kt
**Ships:** two

# NIKI CLASS

**Type:** corvette (FS)
**Country:** Greece
**Displacement:** 732 tons full load
**Dimensions:** length 70m (229.7ft); beam 8.2m (26.9ft); draught 2.7m (8.6ft)
**Gun armament:** twin Breda 40mm (1.57in)
**Torpedoes:** four 324mm (12.75in) single tubes for Honeywell Mk 46
**Performance:** maximum speed 19.6kt
**Range:** 4,443km (2,760 miles) at 15kt
**Ships:** five

# KHUKRI CLASS

**Type:** corvette (FSG)
**Country:** India
**Displacement:** 1,350 tons full load
**Dimensions:** length 91m (298.6ft); beam 10.5m (34.4ft); draught 2.5m (8.2ft)
**Gun armament:** one USSR AK 76mm (3in)/60; twin AK 630 30mm (1.18in)/65
**Missile armament:** one or two twin SS-N-2D Styx SSM launchers; SA-N-5 Grail SAM launcher
**Aircraft:** platform only for one Chetak
**Electronics:** air search; air/surface search; navigation; fire control radar systems
**Performance:** maximum speed 25kt
**Range:** 6,440km (4,000 miles) at 16kt
**Ships:** four

# BAYANDOR CLASS

**Type:** corvette (FS)
**Country:** Iran
**Displacement:** 1,135 tons full load
**Dimensions:** length 84m (275.6ft); beam 10.1m (33.1ft); draught 3.1m (10.2ft)
**Gun armament:** two US 76mm (3in)/50 Mk 3/4; twin Bofors 40mm (1.57in); two Oerlikon GAM-B01 20mm (0.79in); two 12.7mm (0.5in) MGs
**Performance:** maximum speed 20kt
**Range:** 7,728km (4,800 miles) at 12kt
**Ships:** two

# EITHNE CLASS

**Type:** corvette (FSH)
**Country:** Ireland
**Displacement:** 1,910 tons full load
**Dimensions:** length 80.8m (265ft); beam 12m (39.4ft); draught 4.3m (14.1ft)
**Gun armament:** one Bofors 57mm (2.24in); two Rheinmetall 20mm (0.79in)
**Aircraft:** one SA 365F Dauphin 2 helicopter
**Performance:** maximum speed 20kt
**Range:** 11,270km (7,000 miles) at 15kt
**Ships:** one

# EILAT CLASS

**Type:** corvette (FSG)
**Country:** Israel
**Displacement:** 1,227 tons full load
**Dimensions:** length 85.6m (280.8ft); beam 11.9m (39ft); draught 3.2m (10.5ft)
**Gun armament:** one OTO Melara 76mm (3in); two Sea Vulcan 25mm (1in) CIWS
**Missile armament:** two quad Harpoon SSM launchers; two vertical SAM launchers
**Torpedoes:** two triple 324mm (12.75in) tubes for Honeywell Mk 46
**Aircraft:** one Dauphin SA 366G helicopter
**Performance:** maximum speed 33kt
**Range:** 5,635km (3,500 miles) at 17kt
**Ships:** two

# MINERVA CLASS

**Type:** corvette (FSG)
**Country:** Italy
**Displacement:** 1,285 tons full load
**Dimensions:** length 86.6m (284.1ft); beam 10.5m (34.5ft); draught 3.2m (10.5ft)
**Gun armament:** one OTO Melara 76mm (3in)/62 compact
**Missile armament:** fitted for SSM launchers; octuple Albatross SAM launcher
**Torpedoes:** two triple 324mm (12.75in) tubes for Honeywell Mk 46
**Performance:** maximum speed 24kt
**Range:** 5,635km (3,500 miles) at 18kt
**Ships:** eight

# QAHIR CLASS

**Type:** corvette (FSG)
**Country:** Oman
**Displacement:** 1,450 tons full load
**Dimensions:** length 83.7m (274.6ft); beam 11.5m (37.7ft); draught 3.6m (11.8ft)
**Gun armament:** one OTO Melara 76mm (3in)/62; two Oerlikon 20mm (0.79in)
**Missile armament:** eight Exocet SSM launchers; octuple SAM launcher
**Aircraft:** platform for one helicopter
**Performance:** maximum speed 19.6kt
**Range:** 4,443km (2,760 miles) at 15kt
**Ships:** two; *Qahir Al Amwaj* (Q31), *illustrated below,* and *Al Muazzer* (Q32)

# PO HANG CLASS

**Type:** corvette (FS)
**Country:** Korea, South
**Displacement:** 1,220 tons full load
**Dimensions:** length 88.3m (289.7ft); beam 10m (32.8ft); draught 2.9m (9.5ft)
**Gun armament:** one OTO Melara 76mm (3in)/62 compact; two twin 30mm (1.18in) or four Breda 40mm (1.57in)
**Missile armament:** two Aerospatiale MM 38 Exocet SSM launchers
**Torpedoes:** two triple 324mm (12.75in) tubes for Honeywell Mk 46
**Performance:** maximum speed 32kt
**Range:** 6,440km (4,000 miles) at 15kt
**Ships:** twenty-three

# NANUCHKA I CLASS

**Type:** corvette (FSG)
**Country:** Russia and associated states
**Displacement:** 900 tons full load
**Dimensions:** length 59.3m (194.5ft); beam 12.6m (41.3ft); draught 2.4m (7.9ft)
**Gun armament:** twin 57mm (2.24in)/80 AA
**Missile armament:** two triple SSM launchers; twin SAM launcher
**Performance:** maximum speed 36kt
**Range:** 4,025km (2,500 miles) at 12kt
**Ships:** fourteen

# TARANTUL II CLASS

**Type:** corvette (FSG)
**Country:** Russia and associated states
**Displacement:** 455 tons full load
**Dimensions:** length 56.1m (184.1ft); beam 11.5m (37.7ft); draught 2.5m (8.2ft)
**Gun armament:** one 76mm (3in)/60; two 30mm (1.18in)/65
**Missile armament:** two twin SSM launchers; quad SAM launcher
**Performance:** maximum speed 36kt
**Range:** 2,656km (1,650 miles) at 14kt
**Ships:** eighteen

# BADR CLASS

**Type:** corvette (FS)
**Country:** Saudi Arabia
**Displacement:** 1,038 tons full load
**Dimensions:** length 74.7m (245ft); beam 9.6m (31.5ft); draught 2.7m (8.9ft)
**Gun armament:** one 76mm (3in); one 20mm (0.79in); two Oerlikon 20mm (0.79in)
**Missile armament:** two quad McDonnell Douglas Harpoon SSM launchers
**Torpedoes:** two triple 324mm (12.75in) tubes for Honeywell Mk 46
**Performance:** maximum speed 30kt
**Range:** 6,440km (4,000 miles) at 20kt
**Ships:** four

# VICTORY CLASS

**Type:** corvette (FSG)
**Country:** Singapore
**Displacement:** 550 tons full load
**Dimensions:** length 62.4m (204.7ft); beam 8.5m (27.9ft); draught 3.1m (10.2ft)
**Gun armament:** one OTO Melara 76mm (3in)/62 Super Rapid
**Missile armament:** two quad Harpoon SSM launchers; one SAM launcher
**Torpedoes:** two triple 324mm (12.75in) tubes for Whitehead A 244S
**Performance:** maximum speed 35kt
**Range:** 6,440km (4,000 miles) at 18kt
**Ships:** six

# GÖTEBORG CLASS

**Type:** corvette (FS)
**Country:** Sweden
**Displacement:** 399 tons full load
**Dimensions:** length 57m (187ft); beam 8m (26.2ft); draught 2m (6.6ft)
**Gun armament:** one Bofors 57mm (2.24in)/70; one Bofors 40mm (1.57in)/70
**Missile armament:** four twin launchers for SSMs
**Torpedoes:** four 400mm (15.75in) tubes
**Performance:** maximum speed 32kt
**Ships:** four

# STOCKHOLM CLASS

**Type:** corvette (FS)
**Country:** Sweden
**Displacement:** 335 tons full load
**Dimensions:** length 50m (164ft); beam 6.8m (22.3ft); draught 1.9m (6.2ft)
**Gun armament:** one Bofors 57mm (2.24in)/70; one Bofors 40mm (1.57in)/70
**Missile armament:** four twin launchers for SSMs
**Torpedoes:** two 533mm (21in) tubes; four 400mm (15.75in) tubes
**Performance:** maximum speed 32kt
**Ships:** two

# KHAMRONSIN CLASS

**Type:** corvette (FS)
**Country:** Thailand
**Displacement:** 475 tons full load
**Dimensions:** length 62m (203.4ft); beam 8.2m (26.9ft); draught 2.5m (8.2ft)
**Gun armament:** one OTO Melara 76mm (3in)/62; twin Breda 30mm (1.18in)/70
**Torpedoes:** two triple launchers for MUSL Stingray
**Performance:** maximum speed 25kt
**Range:** 4,025km (2,500 miles) at 15kt
**Ships:** three

# RATTANAKOSIN CLASS

**Type:** corvette (FSG)
**Country:** Thailand
**Displacement:** 960 tons full load
**Dimensions:** length 76.8m (252ft); beam 9.6m (31.5ft); draught 2.4m (8ft)
**Gun armament:** one OTO Melara 76mm (3in)/62; twin Breda 40mm (1.57in)/70; two Oerlikon 20mm (0.79in)
**Missile armament:** two quad Harpoon SSM launchers; octuple SAM launcher
**Torpedoes:** two triple US Mk 32 324mm (12.75in) tubes for MUSL Stingray
**Performance:** maximum speed 26kt
**Range:** 4,830km (3,000 miles) at 16kt
**Ships:** two

# PATROL FORCES

Although overshadowed by the more illustrious larger warships, the smaller combatants have been by far the most numerous ships to have been built since the conclusion of the Second World War. What we have been able to include here is only a small representation to illustrate the widespread diversity of these effective and versatile small craft.

Hundreds of vessels of different types have been launched, with various missions, but most of these small craft fall into two general classes: fast attack craft and coastal patrol. Also included historically were the small gunboats, river craft and small escort ships that were not large enough to be classed as corvettes, although the specialist mine craft which really fall into a separate category of their own are not included.

Immediately after the Second World War, most of the many hundreds of small combatants that had been built during the war years were retired and broken up, or given away to smaller powers which were able to keep them in service for the next couple of decades. In this period, the Soviets lead the way with the construction of new small craft such as the Komar class fast attack missile boats, which were built in their hundreds from the mid 1950s and which were followed by the equally numerous Osa class.

The Soviet programme completely overshadowed the handful of fast attack craft built by the United States. The most interesting of these craft, the Pegasus class hydrofoils commissioned in the late 1970s, were retired in 1993. The USA also built a wide range of small riverine craft for the Vietnam War, including the aluminium Swift boats.

It was America's foes who were able to operate their small craft to a much greater effect, attacking US destroyers, particularly the Iranians in the Persian Gulf.

The UK deploys two classes of patrol craft to fulfil the task of maintaining the integrity of national waters: the Archer class, and the Peacock class. Both of these classes combine their duties with the role of training in peacetime.

The three Peacock large patrol craft vessels were ordered to replace the withdrawn Ton class vessels. To this end, 75 per cent of the cost was met by the Hong Kong government in order to maintain the Royal Navy's presence in the surrounding territorial waters.

Fishery protection in UK national waters is conducted by two classes of offshore patrol vessels, the Castle class and the Island class, which are also responsible for the protection of the oil and gas fields in the North Sea.

# FREMANTLE CLASS

**Type:** large patrol craft (PP)
**Country:** Australia
**Displacement:** 245 tons full load
**Dimensions:** length 41.8m (137.1ft); beam 7.1m (23.3ft); draught 1.8m (5.9ft)
**Gun armament:** one Bofors AN4 40mm (1.57in); two 12.7mm (0.5in) MGs
**Mortars:** one 81mm (3.19in)
**Performance:** maximum speed 30kt
**Range:** 7,728km (4,800 miles)
**Ships:** fifteen

# AHMAD EL FATEH CLASS

**Type:** fast attack craft (FAC)
**Country of origin:** Bahrain
**Displacement:** 259 tons full load
**Dimensions:** length 44.9m (147.3ft); beam 7m (22.9ft); draught 2.5m (8.2ft)
**Gun armament:** one OTO Melara 76mm (3in)/62; twin Breda 40mm (1.57in)/70; three 7.62 mm (0.3in)
**Missile armament:** two twin Aerospatiale MM 40 Exocet SSM launchers
**Performance:** maximum speed 40kt
**Range:** 2,576km (1,600 miles) at 16kt
**Ships:** four

# HAINAN CLASS

**Type:** fast attack craft (FAC)
**Country of origin:** China
**Displacement:** 392 tons full load
**Dimensions:** length 58.8m (192.8ft); beam 7.2m (23.6ft); draught 2.2m (7.2ft)
**Gun armament:** two twin China 57mm (2.24in)/70; two twin USSR 25mm (1in)
**Mortars:** four RBU 1200 anti-submarine
**Electronics:** Pot Head or Skin Head surface search, hull-mounted sonar
**Performance:** maximum speed 30.5kt
**Range:** 2,093km (1,300 miles) at 15kt
**Ships:** ninety-five

# RAMADAN CLASS

**Type:** fast attack craft (FAC)
**Country:** Egypt
**Displacement:** 307 tons full load
**Dimensions:** length 52m (170.6ft); beam 7.6m (25ft); draught 2.3m (7.5ft)
**Gun armament:** one OTO Melara 76mm (3in); twin Breda 40mm (1.57in)/70
**Missile armament:** four OTO Melara/Matra Otomat Mk 1 SSM launchers
**Performance:** maximum speed 40kt
**Range:** 2,576km (1,600 miles) at 16kt
**Ships:** six, including *Hettein* (680), which is *illustrated right*

# P 400 CLASS

**Type:** fast attack craft (FAC)
**Country of origin:** France
**Displacement:** 454 tons full load
**Dimensions:** length 54.5m (178.6ft); beam 8m (26.2ft); draught 2.5m (8.2ft)
**Gun armament:** one Bofors 40mm (1.57in)/60; one Giat 20F2 20mm (0.79in); two 12.7mm (0.5in) MGs
**Electronics:** Racal Decca 1226 surface search
**Performance:** maximum speed 24.5kt
**Range:** 6,762km (4,200 miles) at 15kt
**Ships:** ten, including *L'Audacieuse* (P 682), which is *illustrated right*

# ALBATROS CLASS

**Type:** fast attack craft (FAC)
**Country of origin:** Germany
**Displacement:** 398 tons full load
**Dimensions:** length 57.6m (189ft); beam 7.8m (25.6ft); draught 2.6m (8.5ft)
**Gun armament:** two OTO Melara 76mm (3in)/62 compact
**Missile armament:** two twin Aerospatiale MM 38 Exocet SSM launchers
**Torpedoes:** two 533mm (21in) aft tubes
**Performance:** maximum speed 40kt
**Range:** 2,093km (1,300 miles) at 30kt
**Ships:** ten, including *Falke* (P 6112), which is *illustrated right*

# SPARVIERO CLASS

**Type:** hydrofoil (PHM)
**Country:** Italy
**Displacement:** 60.6 tons full load
**Dimensions:** length 24.6m (80.7ft); beam 7m (23.1ft); draught 4.4m (14.4ft)
**Gun armament:** one OTO Melara 76mm (3in)/62 compact
**Missile armament:** four OTO Melara/Matra Otomat Teseo Mk 2 SSM launchers
**Performance:** maximum speed 48kt when foil-borne
**Range:** 644km (400 miles) at 45kt
**Ships:** six; *Sparviero* (P 420), *illustrated below,* has been decommissioned

# HAUK CLASS

**Type:** fast attack craft (FAC)
**Country of origin:** Norway
**Displacement:** 148 tons full load
**Dimensions:** length 36.5m (120ft); beam 6.1m (20ft); draught 1.5m (5ft)
**Gun armament:** one Bofors 40mm (1.57in)/70; one Rheinmetall 20mm (0.79in)
**Missile armament:** six Kongsberg Penguin Mk 2 Mod 5 SSM launchers; twin Simbad SAM launchers for Matra Mistral
**Torpedoes:** two 533mm (21in) tubes
**Performance:** maximum speed 32kt
**Range:** 708km (440 miles) at 30kt
**Ships:** fourteen

# VELARDE CLASS

**Type:** fast attack craft (FAC)
**Country of origin:** Peru
**Displacement:** 560 tons full load
**Dimensions:** length 64m (210ft); beam 8.4m (27.4ft); draught 1.6m (5.2ft)
**Gun armament:** one OTO Melara 76mm (3in)/62; twin Breda 40mm (1.57in)/70
**Missile armament:** four Aerospatiale MM 38 Exocet SSM launchers
**Performance:** maximum speed 37kt
**Range:** 4,025km (2,500 miles) at 16kt
**Ships:** six, including *Herrera* (CM 24), which is *illustrated below*

# OSA II CLASS

**Type:** fast attack craft (FAC)
**Country of origin:** Russia and associated states
**Displacement:** 245 tons full load
**Dimensions:** length 38.6m (126.6ft); beam 7.6m (24.9ft); draught 2.7m (8.9ft)
**Gun armament:** two twin 30mm (1.18in)/65
**Missile armament:** four SS-N-2B/C SSM launchers; SA-N-5 Grail SAM launchers in some craft only
**Performance:** maximum speed 37kt
**Range:** 805km (500 miles) at 35kt
**Ships:** twelve

# AL SIDDIQ CLASS

**Type:** fast attack craft (FAC)
**Country of origin:** Saudi Arabia
**Displacement:** 478 tons full load
**Dimensions:** length 58.1m (190.5ft); beam 8.1m (26.5ft); draught 2m (6.6ft)
**Gun armament:** one FMC/OTO Melara 76mm (3in)/62 Mk 75 Mod 0; one GE/GD six-barrelled Vulcan Phalanx 20mm (0.79in); two Oerlikon 20mm (0.79in)/80; two 81mm (3.2in) mortars; two 40mm (1.57in) grenade launchers
**Missile armament:** two twin McDonnell Douglas Harpoon SSM launchers
**Performance:** maximum speed 38kt
**Range:** 4,669km (2,900 miles) at 14kt
**Ships:** nine, including *Al Siddiq* (511), which is *illustrated right*

# CASTLE CLASS

**Type:** offshore patrol vessel (PP)
**Country:** United Kingdom
**Displacement:** 1,427 tons full load
**Dimensions:** length 81m (265.7ft); beam 11.5m (37.7ft); draught 3.6m (11.8ft)
**Gun armament:** one DES/Lawrence Scott Mk 1 30mm (1.18in)/75
**Aircraft:** platform for operating Westland Sea King or Lynx
**Performance:** maximum speed 19.5kt
**Range:** 16,100km (10,000 miles) at 12kt
**Ships:** two, including *Leeds Castle* (P 258), which is *illustrated right*

# PEACOCK CLASS

**Type:** large patrol craft (PG)
**Country of origin:** United Kingdom
**Displacement:** 690 tons full load
**Dimensions:** length 62.6m (204.1ft); beam 10m (32.8ft); draught 2.7m (8.9ft)
**Gun armament:** one OTO Melara 76mm (3in)/62 compact; four FN 7.62mm (0.3in) MGs
**Performance:** maximum speed 25kt
**Range:** 4,025km (2,500 miles) at 17kt
**Ships:** three, including *Peacock* (P 239), which is *illustrated right*

# NAVAL WEAPONRY

This brief chapter highlights just some of the vast array of onboard weapons of various type and category.

**Anti-submarine weapons:** include depth charges, which are usually launched from rails over the vessel's stern. Larger warships, including aircraft carriers, are fitted with multiple rocket launchers known as RBUs, from the Russian **R**akatnaya **B**ombometnaya **U**stanovka. These multi-barrelled rocket launchers were developed from the ahead-firing principle and can fire high-explosive charges with either depth or influence fusing; most can be trained in azimuth and elevation. Such charges are immune to torpedo countermeasures, and if influence fusing is used they will not affect sonar performance as they cannot detonate unless they make contact with a submarine's magnetic signature.

**Naval guns:** the largest naval guns to have entered service postwar were the 406mm (16in) guns fitted to the US Iowa class battleships. The largest Soviet equivalent of the period was the 152.4mm (6in)/57 calibre gun that was fitted in triple mounts in its Sverdlov class cruisers.

**Above:** the US Navy Iowa class battleship M*ISSOURI* firing her 406mm (16in) guns

**Left:** the Soviet RBU-1000 launcher comprises two vertical rows of three automatically reloadable tubes (Aldino)

**Torpedoes:** are used against both surface and submarine targets, launched from trainable tubes in surface warships and from fixed tubes in submarines. Propulsion is provided by steam or electricity, at speeds of approximately 28–45kt, with an effective range from about 3.2–16km (2–10 miles). Guidance may be either preset (straight or pattern-running) or acoustic homing. Their warheads are either high-explosive or nuclear; torpedoes were the first Soviet weapons with a nuclear capacity.

One popular ship-launched anti-submarine weapon system of the past few decades has been the American Honeywell RUR-5A ASROC (**A**nti-**S**ubmarine **Roc**ket) system, introduced in 1962 by the US Navy. This ballistic weapon is aimed and launched from a dedicated Mk 16 octuple launcher or Mk 10 and 26 twin SAM/ASROC launchers, on information supplied by the ship's sonar system via the underwater weapons fire-control system.

*Above:* three partially-exposed 533mm (21in) torpedoes in the starboard quadruple torpedo bank of a Kirov I class frigate (Aldino)

**Surface-to-surface missiles:** in service since the 1950s, these have since been developed as the SS-N-2 Styx, providing an anti-ship missile capability for small combat craft in the coastal defence role. It had an initial range of 46km (28.5 miles), and until the French Exocet, operational from 1973, and the American Harpoon of 1977, was the most widely used anti-ship missile.

The Aerospatiale MM 38 Exocet is the most widely produced anti-ship missile of western origins. Designed in the late 1960s, it began to enter service in 1974. The missile is launched towards the target on data provided by the launch ship's sensors and fire-control system and cruises at low level until some 10km (6.2 miles) from the anticipated target position, when the monopulse active seeker head is turned on.

The McDonnell Douglas RGM-84A Harpoon is the western world's most important ship-launched anti-ship missile, conceived in the late 1960s as a capable but comparatively cheap weapon, emphasising reliability rather than outright performance in all respects but electronic capability and range. The missile can be fired in both range and bearing mode, allowing for the late activation of the active radar as a means of reducing the chances of the missile being detected through its own emissions.

***Above:*** *an Exocet MM 40 medium range anti-ship missile being fired (Aldino)*
***Below:*** *a medium/long-range anti-ship Harpoon missile (Aldino)*

Ship-launched, air-breathing cruise missiles such as the Soviet SS-N-3 Shaddock were developed in parallel; the later SS-N-12 Sandbox, part of the Kiev class aircraft carrier's armoury, was twice as fast as the Shaddock, having a range of 555km [345 miles]). All of these systems are turbojet propelled.

Its western counterpart is the General Dynamics BGM-109B Tomahawk, which has a speed of 805km/h (500mph) and a range of 467km (290 miles). It carries a conventional warhead and an active radar seeker derived from that of the Harpoon. A French-Italian designed medium-range anti-ship missile, the OTO Melara / Matra Otomat family, includes the Otomat. This is launched from a self-contained container-launcher and is a capable air-breathing weapon that cruises at 250m (820ft) before descending to 20m (66ft) in the closing stages of the attack.

**Surface-to-air missiles:** most of the Soviet missiles of this type were developed from land-based systems. Examples are the small SA-N-5, which can either be shoulder-held or fired from a four-missile launch rack, and the SA-N-6, which has an anti-cruise missile capability and is vertically launched from a below-deck rotary magazine with eight missiles per launcher. They were originally fitted in one of the Kara class cruisers. The SA-N-7 was introduced in 1981, when two launchers were fitted to the Sovremenny class destroyers, combined with six Front Dome radar directors. All of these are solid-fuel rockets with conventional warheads.

Western equivalents include the Raytheon RIM-7M Sea Sparrow and the General Dynamics RIM-66A/B Standard. The Sea Sparrow, developed in the early 1960s, has variants including the NATO system, which has capabilities against low-flying targets. Combining a digital fire-control system and powered tracker and illuminator, it is fired from a Mk 29 octuple launcher. The RIM-66A entered service in 1968 with the Mk 27 Mod 0 solid-propellant rocket and is usually associated with the Mk 11/12 twin launcher (42 missiles), Mk 13 single launcher (40 missiles), or Mk 22 single launcher (16 missiles). The type also has a horizon-limited surface-to-surface capability and a proximity and impact-fused high-explosive warhead.

*The background illustration is of the short-range anti-missile surface-to-air Sea Wolf weapon system. This third generation of Sea Wolf is vertically launched and is capable of intercepting a 114mm (4.5in) shell. The system is fitted in the Type 23 frigates of the Royal Navy with 32 missiles installed in vertical sealed canisters ready for firing. Developed by BAe Dynamics, it was the first operational anti-missile ship defence weapon system and has proved its efficiency against fast sea-skimming and high-angle supersonic missiles. The initial version of Sea Wolf was successfully deployed in the Falklands war (1982)*

# GLOSSARY

| | |
|---|---|
| **AEW** | **A**irborne **E**arly **W**arning |
| **A/S, ASW** | **A**nti-**S**ubmarine (**W**arfare) |
| **ASM** | **A**ir-to-**S**urface **M**issile |
| **ASROC** | **A**nti-**S**ubmarine **ROC**ket |
| **BPDMS** | **B**ase **P**oint **D**efence **M**issile **S**ystem |
| **CIWS** | **C**lose-**I**n-**W**eapons **S**ystem |
| **DP** | **D**epth **C**harge |
| **DCT** | **D**epth **C**harge **T**hrower |
| **ECM** | **E**lectronic **C**ounter**M**easures |
| **ELINT** | **EL**ectronic **INT**elligence |
| **ESM** | **E**lectronic **S**upport **M**easures |
| **EW** | **E**lectronic **W**arfare |
| **FLIR** | **F**orward **L**ooking **I**nfra-red **R**adar |
| **FRAM** | **F**leet **R**ehabilitation **A**nd **M**odernisation programme |
| **GFCS** | **G**un **F**ire **C**ontrol **S**ystem |
| **GMLS** | **G**uided **M**issile **L**aunch **S**ystem |
| **GWS** | **G**uided **W**eapons **S**ystem |
| **LAMPS** | **L**ight **A**irborne **M**ulti-**P**urpose **S**ystem |
| **LRMP** | **L**ong-**R**ange **M**aritime **P**atrol |
| **MDF** | **M**aritime **D**efence **F**orce |
| **MFCS** | **M**issile **F**ire **C**ontrol **S**ystem |
| **MG** | **M**achine **G**un |
| **MIRV** | **M**ultiple, **I**ndependently targetable **R**e-entry **V**ehicle |
| **PDMS** | **P**oint **D**efence **M**issile **S**ystem |
| **RBU** | Anti-Submarine Rocket Launcher (see page 150) |
| **SAM** | **S**urface-to-**A**ir **M**issile |
| **SAR** | **S**earch **A**nd **R**escue |
| **SATCOM** | **SAT**ellite **COM**munications |
| **SINS** | **S**hip's **I**nertial **N**avigation **S**ystem |
| **SLCM** | **S**hip-**L**aunched **C**ruise **M**issile |
| **SLEP** | **S**ervice **L**ife **E**xtension **P**rogramme |
| **SSM** | **S**urface-to-**S**urface **M**issile |
| **STIR** | **S**urveillance **T**arget **I**ndicator **R**adar |
| **VDS** | **V**ariable **D**epth **S**onar |
| **VLS** | **V**ertical **L**aunch **S**ystem |
| **V/STOL** | **V**ertical or **S**hort **T**ake-**O**ff/**L**anding |

# INDEX OF VESSELS AND CLASSES